HEALING YOUR
GRIEF ABOUT AGING

Also by Alan Wolfelt and Kirby Duvall:

Healing After Job Loss:
100 Practical Ideas

Healing Your Grieving Heart
When Someone You Care About Has Alzheimer's:
100 Practical Ideas for Families, Friends, and Caregivers

Healing Your Grieving Body:
100 Physical Practices for Mourners

Also by Alan Wolfelt:

Creating Meaningful Funeral Ceremonies:
A Guide for Families

Healing the Adult Child's Grieving Heart:
100 Practical Ideas After Your Parent Dies

Healing a Friend's Grieving Heart:
100 Practical Ideas for Helping Someone
You Love Through Loss

The Journey Through Grief:
Reflections on Healing

Understanding Your Grief:
Ten Essential Touchstones for Finding
Hope and Healing Your Heart

The Wilderness of Grief: Finding Your Way

Loving from the Outside In,
Mourning from the Inside Out

Companion Press is dedicated to the education and support of both the bereaved and bereavement caregivers. We believe that those who companion the bereaved by walking with them as they journey in grief have a wondrous opportunity: to help others embrace and grow through grief—and to lead fuller, more deeply-lived lives themselves because of this important ministry.

Companion
PRESS

For a complete catalog and ordering information, visit:

Companion Press
The Center for Loss and Life Transition
3735 Broken Bow Road
Fort Collins, CO 80526
(970) 226-6050
www.centerforloss.com

HEALING YOUR GRIEF ABOUT AGING

•

100 PRACTICAL IDEAS ON GROWING OLDER WITH CONFIDENCE, MEANING, AND GRACE

•

ALAN D. WOLFELT, PH.D.
KIRBY J. DUVALL, M.D.

Companion
P R E S S

Fort Collins, Colorado

An imprint of the Center for Loss and Life Transition

Companion Press is an imprint of the
Center for Loss and Life Transition,
3735 Broken Bow Road, Fort Collins, Colorado 80526
970-226-6050
www.centerforloss.com

Companion Press books may be purchased in bulk for sales promotions, premiums or fundraisers. Please contact the publisher at the above address for more information.

Printed in the United States of America

17 16 15 14 13 12   5 4 3 2 1

ISBN: 978-1-61722-171-2

CONTENTS

INTRODUCTION

A simple truth is that from the day we enter into this world, we start to age. To be human means to grow older each day we are on this earth. We begin and we end. However, we have infinite choices about what comes in between.

We know whereof we speak. Perhaps you have heard the saying, "You teach what you need to know." Well, we have both become aware of the need to know about the journey of aging because it is our journey too. As we write this, we are both in our late fifties. We have both been faced with becoming adult orphans, as all of our parents have now died. We have also experienced the sudden deaths of friends and colleagues younger than we are. In addition, we have both had age-related health challenges, including the loss of some of our energy. Perhaps some of our experiences are familiar to you. Yes, we are all on this path together and we need not walk alone.

Yet we have chosen not to be passive bystanders in the process of aging. We have learned that if we say yes to the natural progress of aging, we have the opportunity to do so with grace and even joy. On the other hand, if we fight it or try to be 25 when we are really 45, we will probably find we've plunged ourselves into mid-life crises.

Ageism in North America

Our bodies often remind us we are changing long before our minds do (at least that has been the case for us!). Our bodies declare the realities of aging and introduce us to a heightened awareness of our mortality. Even as our bodies speak to us, our contemporary culture's youth obsession screams. We worship the idea of perpetual youth, so we struggle against the passage into becoming a "senior citizen." The huge anti-aging trend reinforces the idea that growing old is to be avoided at all costs—and cost it does!

At our fingertips, we now have Botox shots that paralyze our face muscles so we look more youthful and Restylane injections that fill sags and reduce wrinkles. We have hair-coloring, face-lifting, and teeth-whitening. We have garments that put body parts back where they used to be. We are surrounded by advertising that has us believing we can be "younger next year" or "regain our youth" or, even better, "live to be 150."

The result is that ageism is alive and well in North America. Ageism is the term used to describe a societal pattern of widely held devaluative attitudes, beliefs, and stereotypes based on chronological age. If you're supposed to avoid wrinkles, gray hair, baldness, or anything that suggests you are getting older, how can you embrace the present and grow old gracefully? In a sense, ageism is an attempt to distance oneself from the realities of aging, illness, death, and grief.

Grace

The knowing that you are not alone, that you are always accompanied. Grace expands your will by giving you a courage you did not have before. Grace invites you to embrace your natural aging and discover the wisdom inherent in the process.

Yes, in our culture we tend to avoid the realities of aging, which ultimately leads to the greatest that-which-shall-not-be-named: death. But as long as we internalize and try to live out society's attempt to go around aging instead of through it, we give up our precious opportunity to have grace and strength in the face of what aging brings into our lives.

We believe that our need to control is what underlies this tendency to "fight" the normal aging process. After all, you don't have to grieve and mourn if you can stay "in control." Most North Americans don't like losing control.

To grieve and mourn the losses of aging

Yet even though we may struggle for control for as long as we possibly can, aging inexorably brings us loss and grief. We cannot overcome aging and death. As our bodies change, we lose function and, society tells us, beauty. We lose our careers and sometimes our houses, our lifestyles, our finances. Our children grow up and move away. And one by one, our friends and family members begin to take their leave from us here on earth.

Especially in the beginning, the losses of aging can be ambiguous. Many occur over a long duration of time (up to 20 to 30 years or more), go socially unrecognized, and are surrounded by uncertainty. For example, you may have begun to experience short-term memory problems years ago. While these lapses did not radically compromise your ability to function, they may have more subtly affected your ability to communicate with loved ones, participate in social activities, and share intimacy. Relationships and roles, future dreams, and certainly your sense of normalcy may have slowly deteriorated. Or there may have come a time when you could no longer play basketball, run, and do vigorous activities.

You may feel, "I just can't do so many of the things that I used to be able to do" or "My mind can no longer work like it used to." You might feel like you're not the same person anymore. You may feel like you are still twenty, but your mind may write checks your body cannot cash anymore. What was once normal is now changed.

And so we can't help but grieve. *Grief* is the constellation of internal thoughts and feelings we have when we lose something or someone we love or deeply value. Grief is the anxiety, bewilderment, anger, sadness, and other emotions we feel on the inside. We are here to tell you that grief in aging is normal and necessary—so necessary, in fact, that it is only by embracing it that you can go on to live the life you yearn for. *Mourning* is this embrace. It is the acknowledgment and outward expression of your grief. We all grieve as we age, but if we are to live a continued life of confidence, meaning, and grace, we must also mourn.

It is up to you to actively engage in the mourning that aging invites into your life. It is up to you to trust that authentic mourning is how you integrate losses and move through them to what comes next. Then and only then do you have the space for the wisdom that aging urges you to discover and share.

Yes, aging can liberate you from your previous roles and offer you the chance to be authentic, genuine, congruent, and honest. Old age gives you the opportunity to be more of who you've always been.

Our theory of aging

You may be aware that there are a number of theories about the aging process, with academic names ranging from "disengagement theory" to "continuity theory" to "gerotranscendence theory"...and the list goes on. We thought that you, the reader, were entitled to know which theory underlies our beliefs about aging.

We believe in what we like to call the "discernment theory" of aging. We think that as older people, the decisions we make every day have much to do with how our aging experience goes. Being a discerner means you decide what gives your existence quality and meaning. It embraces that, while circumstances will arise that are beyond your control, the journey is truly yours.

Yes, we acknowledge that life hands us many surprises, both happy and sad. We realize that there is much we cannot control. But we also know we have many choices to make as we navigate this phase of our lives. For example, you can choose to be busy and stay active doing things that interest you, or you can disengage and withdraw some—if that is what is satisfying to you. The point is to listen to and trust your deepest wisdom and your strongest yearnings and choose to follow them where they lead.

Growing older invites an awareness of your inherent value while recognizing you are so much more than the sum of your accomplishments or your work product. Growing older invites you to remember the gifts you have to offer your family, friends, and the world around you. As your life moves from the "Surf at Waikiki" to "On Golden Pond," you have the freedom to befriend your aging, experiment with the 100 ways outlined in this resource, or do nothing at all. While aging is inevitable, how you will age is often largely up to you.

Aging invites you to have discernment. When you are "discerning," you are using your hard-earned powers of understanding—intellectual, emotional, and spiritual powers—to distinguish what is good for you and what is not; what is helpful versus unhelpful; what is necessary instead of unnecessary. Growing older gives us time to find the natural rhythms that best suit us. Our hope is that this book will help you discern how to re-imagine your final decades not as a time of dismal, depressing decline, but as one of opportunity and fulfillment, one to truly enjoy and even cherish. We invite you on this journey to befriend aging to the fullest!

How to use this book

We invite you to think of this book as a "User's Guide to Graceful Aging." While there is no one "right way" to grow old, we have attempted to fill these pages with information and ideas that have served us well on our personal journeys as well as research that provides practical applications for you, the reader. The goal of this book is to invite you to make your own journey more purpose-filled and joyful. With seventy million of us Baby Boomers running around, we think this is a much-needed resource and hope you do too.

This common-sense guide explores five domains of aging: *physical, intellectual, emotional, social,* and *spiritual.* We have attempted to provide a holistic framework that lets you examine these five critical areas of the aging process. Thinking of yourself in this holistic way means viewing yourself as a whole being—not a collection of parts. While we have included an important section on befriending the physical challenges of getting older, we were not interested in writing another book solely on exercise and nutrition as the keys to healthy aging. Because while they are indeed fundamental to aging well, we also believe that other vital tasks—like maintaining healthy relationships, serving others, being out in nature, and having a satisfying spiritual life—are just as—if not more—important. We believe that inner and outer aging are interrelated, and this viewpoint is reflected in the contents of these pages. After all, until we have meaning and purpose in our lives, exercise and diet don't mean all that much.

This little book is intended to help you see some of your choices for finding continued meaning, confidence, and grace in your life and give you information, ideas, and tools to help you along your way. We invite you to explore the 100 Ideas and decide which might be a good fit for you now and which to ignore for the time being.

As you flip through these pages, you will also see that each Idea includes a "Carpe Diem," which means, as fans of the movie *Dead*

Poets Society will remember, "seize the day." Our hope is that you not relegate this resource to your shelves but instead keep it handy on your nightstand or desk. Pick it up often and turn to any page; the Carpe Diem suggestion might help you seize the day by giving you an exercise, action, or thought to consider today, right now, right his minute.

We thank you for taking the time to read and reflect on the words that make up this book. We wish you courage, grace, and comfort as you befriend your natural aging process. Please view this little book as an encouraging companion who walks with you. As good friends do, let it fill you with strength as you recite the simple, yet profound, words of Henry Wadsworth Longfellow, who reminds all of us:

> *Age is opportunity no less*
> *Than youth itself, though in another dress,*
> *And as the evening twilight fades away*
> *The sky is filled with*
> *Stars invisible by day.*

What a gift. We hope this little poem will help you shift your focus away from the mere physical manifestations of aging and toward what cannot be taken away: the love we give and receive from those who have brought meaning and purpose to our lives; the wisdom we have gained as we have grown older; and the capacity to pull back and reflect as we renew our meaning and purpose in each day we have left on this earth. Godspeed. We hope to meet you one day.

Befriending the Physical Challenges of Aging

*"Like a lot of fellows around here,
I have a furniture problem.*

My chest has fallen into my drawers."

— Billy Casper

Since it is the physical aspects of aging we tend to notice first, we've made this the first section of the book.

Yet even though our physical challenges might be (or become) significant, if we make the commitment to take care of our aging bodies as well as we can, we will feel better, have more energy, and age more slowly.

If you haven't already, commit to doing everything you can to improve or maintain your physical well-being. Your life will thank you for it.

1.

EMBRACE THE FACT THAT YOU ARE NOT FOREVER YOUNG

"Middle age is always ten years older than you are."
— Jack Benny

• Physical aging, we all know, is relentless from birth to old age. Yet still, it's hard to accept. The face looking back in the mirror doesn't reflect the feelings of the mind looking out, which still feels like that 20-year-old from long ago—young and attractive and strong.

• Aging seems to catch people by surprise. At the time, we were shocked to realize we were having our 50th birthdays. How could that be? We didn't really feel that old.

• Allow yourself to grieve the passing of years. Acknowledge the loss of your youth. Then, draw a mental line in the sand to signify your past and your future. When you are ready, step over the line and embrace your new, aged self. Start afresh from where you stand, right now.

• Nothing is constant but change. You will be happier, healthier, and age more gracefully if you recognize the simple fact that physically you cannot be forever young. But retaining your sense of wonder and enjoying each day—that is attainable.

CARPE DIEM:
What parts of your own aging process have you tried to deny? Make a list. How can you embrace these aspects of your changed self?

2.

THINK TWICE ABOUT AGE-DEFYING PROCEDURES AND PRODUCTS

"There is a fountain of youth: It is your mind, your talents, the creativity you bring to your life and the lives of people you love."

— Sophia Loren

- The market research firm Global Industry Analysts projects that the $80 billion spent on anti-aging products in 2011 in the U.S. will grow to $114 billion in 2015, thanks to Baby Boomers growing older.

- Approach anti-aging products and procedures thoughtfully. Think about what you want to achieve. If you want to turn back time 20 years, that's impossible. Be skeptical and realistic when purchasing a product or dishing out big money for procedures like facelifts or ongoing Botox treatments. Don't fall victim to false promises. The fountain of youth has yet to be found, and anything you do won't last forever.

- Take this opportunity to ask yourself key questions about aging. For example, "Why is it so important for me to look young?" or "What do I think young people have that I don't?" Is what comes up real, or is it reflective of the media's anti-aging messages? Also, consider whether your self-worth has been tied to your appearance and what that means for you moving ahead.

- Be that older person whose eyes sparkle bright from a well-worn face that speaks of living a full life now, today, versus in the fading past. You can redefine what it means to grow old. Make it what you want it to be.

CARPE DIEM:
Bring to mind older people whom you respect. Most likely, they convey a sense of wisdom, peace, and satisfaction in their lives. Set a mental compass to move in their direction.

3.

ADAPT TO A PHYSICAL "NEW NORMAL"

*"Maybe it's true that life begins at 50. But everything
else starts to wear out, fall out, or spread out."*

— Phyllis Diller

- As we age, our bodies change. Seemingly overnight, we can't read the menu or see well driving in the dark. We feel stiff in the mornings and take longer to get moving. When we are physically active, we're more tired the next day or we get injured more easily. Sometimes, chronic illnesses carried in our genes present themselves. Needless to say, we are not who we once were in our glory days.

- Allow yourself to feel sad about your physical losses. Tell someone or journal about your past physical prowess. Own that these achievements are yours, despite the fact that you can no longer perform them.

- When you're ready, move toward accepting your new physical reality. Brainstorm ways to adjust. Buy dimestore readers and carry them with you. Take time in the morning to stretch before heading out the door. Remember that you can't do eight hours of yard work anymore. Learn to manage your diabetes, arthritis, or high blood pressure.

- When you resist these physical effects of aging, you feel frustrated. Maybe, like others, you get stuck in inaction. Tap into the relief that comes with saying, "Maybe I can no longer run 10ks, but I could run or walk a 5k."

- Try out a new, ageless sport like tennis, skiing, golf, kayaking, sailing, or water aerobics. Who knows, you might still be doing it in your 80s.

CARPE DIEM:
Take inventory of your aging body. What is harder now
than it used to be? What new challenges have cropped up?
Redefine your physical abilities and find a doable solution
or physical outlet that complements your 'new normal.'

4.

PLAN FOR WELLNESS

"As I see it, every day you do one of two things:
build health or produce disease in yourself."
— Adelle Davis

• Wellness is defined as the pursuit of optimal health through responsible behavior choices. It goes beyond the conventional definition of health, i.e., the absence of disease. The dimensions of wellness include physical, emotional, spiritual, intellectual, and social health.

• The first phase of wellness is awareness. Become aware of your health by doing a self-assessment to consider where you are on the wellness continuum.

• The next phase is education. Seek out information about how to improve your health. Your physician, reputable books and websites, and other health professionals are good sources of this information.

• Finally, take action on an intervention that can help improve the current state of your health.

• Making a plan helps you act to improve your health. Write down your wellness goals and tell someone about them. For example, tell your spouse of your plan to eliminate fatty foods from your diet in order to lower your cholesterol and heart attack risk.

• Work in rewards to keep yourself motivated—they can be simple, like coffee with a friend after working out.

CARPE DIEM:
Take inventory of how you are doing in each of the five wellness dimensions. Brainstorm solutions for the one that's least active.

5.

SCHEDULE PREVENTIVE HEALTH SCREENINGS AND CHECKS

*"If we could give every individual the right amount of
nourishment and exercise, not too little and not too much,
we would have found the safest way to health."*

— Hippocrates

- Due for a tune up? Just like your car, your body needs regular maintenance. Health screenings are good checks to make sure your various bodily systems are functioning well. Talk to your doctor about which tests are right for you.

- Keep your shots up to date. Adults need a tetanus-diphtheria booster every 10 years. Consider a flu shot each year. If you are over 65, also consider a pneumonia vaccine. If you have a chronic disease, get one sooner. Ask about the shingles vaccine as well.

- There are specific health screenings for men and women. For example, men over 50 should consider a prostate cancer screening. Breast cancer is the second most common cause of death for women. Women should receive a physical breast check annually and after age 40, a mammogram. Women should also get regular Pap smears, which can detect cervical cancer.

- Don't forget all the standard tests that come with annual visits— cholesterol and blood pressure for heart disease, insulin check for diabetes, and more. If you haven't had an annual exam in the last year, schedule one today.

- Having one person who knows your medical history and can watch for changes is critical as you age.

CARPE DIEM:
Are you current on your cancer screenings? Visit the American Cancer Society website at www.cancer.org and search the phrase "screening by age" to see a list of what's needed and when.

6.

NOURISH YOUR AGING BODY

"The best way to detoxify is to stop putting
toxic things into your body."
— Andrew Weil

- Every time you open a health magazine there's new advice on which foods or nutrients you should be getting as you age. How do you sort through it all? Here are four well-tested ones that many of us don't get enough of:

- Fish oil (omega 3 fatty acid). Omega 3 lowers blood pressure and reduces the risk of death, heart attack, dangerous heart rhythms, and strokes. It also reduces inflammation and joint pain. Take a supplement daily and eat fish, walnuts, flaxseeds, and heart-healthy vegetable oils like canola, soybean, and olive.

- B12. Vitamin B12 helps make red blood cells and DNA. It also keeps your nervous system working properly. It's mainly found in fish, shellfish, meat, and dairy products. Older people are at risk for low vitamin B12. Multivitamins often don't contain enough B12.

- Calcium. As our bodies age, we can't absorb as much calcium as we used to, making us more susceptible to osteoporosis and bone fractures. Women in menopause are especially at risk.

- Green tea (antioxidants). Green tea has been used to treat ailments for 4,000 years. Recent studies show its high antioxidant content boosts the immune system and reduces infection.

CARPE DIEM:
Add these four nutrients to your daily routine
for better health as you age.

7.

EAT MORE HIGH-FIBER AND HIGH-VITAMIN FOODS

"Stressed spelled backwards is desserts. Coincidence? I think not."
— Anonymous

- As you get older, you may get less hungry. If you've experienced a recent death of a loved one or are grieving the passing of time, your appetite may also be suffering.

- Concentrate on getting adequate fiber, vitamins, and minerals in your diet to maintain your health. A simple way to do this is to eat more fruits and vegetables. Challenge yourself to eat eight servings a day, or more. Fiber is also found in whole grains.

- Another simple way to ensure you are eating healthy foods is to eat whole foods, or foods that are "close to nature." Avoid packaged foods as much as possible. When choosing packaged foods, buy those that have five or fewer ingredients—and words that you recognize.

- Consider a Mediterranean diet. This eating tradition, most common in Greece, Italy, and Spain, is linked to good health. It promotes good fats, like avocados and olive oil, moderate fish and poultry, and plenty of fruits, vegetables, beans, grains, nuts, and seeds.

- Finally, try eating less to live longer. Studies of centenarians found that the majority lived in modest circumstances and ate less than average. Other studies show a reduction in calorie intake increases life expectancy. To decrease your calorie intake, follow the "three-quarters rule" and stop eating when you are three-quarters full.

CARPE DIEM:
The next time you go to the grocery store, select a few fruits or vegetables that you haven't had lately. Try them in a new recipe.

8.

FEED YOUR IMMUNE SYSTEM

"An ounce of prevention is worth a pound of cure."
— Benjamin Franklin

• It's a known scientific fact: as we age, our immune systems become less effective. We suffer from more infections, and our response to infections is more severe.

• As we age, our cells begin to break down. Older cells produce fewer antioxidant enzymes, which are needed to eliminate "free radicals"—a byproduct of cell metabolism that can damage proteins and other molecules in our bodies. One way to combat this is to get more antioxidants through our diets.

• Eat antioxidant-rich foods every day, including berries, red kidney beans, pinto beans, artichoke hearts, prunes, pecans, cherries, apples, and green tea. You might also consider taking an antioxidant supplement that includes the vitamins C, E, and beta-carotene.

• Also, eat your cruciferous veggies, like broccoli and cauliflower. UCLA researchers found that a chemical in broccoli and other cruciferous vegetables switches on enzymes in specific immune cells that combat free radicals, according to a recent article in ScienceDaily.

• More and more, researchers are finding that our guts play a key role in our immunity. Do you have chronic stomachaches or acid reflux? If so, work to solve these issues. One way is to improve your gut flora with probiotics—the healthy bacteria that live in our intestines and stomach. Eat yogurt rich in live cultures, or take a supplement.

• Of course, good food, sleep, and exercise also strengthen immunity.

CARPE DIEM:
On your next grocery shopping trip, pick up
one or two antioxidant-rich foods.

9.

DRINK UP

"I believe that water is the only drink for a wise man."
— Henry David Thoreau

- Did you know that your body is about 60 percent water? No wonder you hear so much about drinking plenty of water! Every system in your body depends on water. Especially if you are focusing on your inward feelings right now, you may not feel thirsty or might forget to drink regularly.

- Even mild dehydration of one to two percent loss of body weight can sap your energy and make you tired. Signs and symptoms of dehydration include excessive thirst, fatigue, headache, dry mouth, little or no urination, muscle weakness, dizziness, and lightheadedness.

- Every day you lose water through sweating (noticeable and unnoticeable), exhaling, urinating, and bowel movements. You need to replace this loss by consuming beverages and foods that contain water—preferably just water and not too much fruit juice or soda. Other factors like exercise, the environment (including heat and humidity), and illnesses or health conditions influence your water needs.

- How much water do you need? At least four to five cups a day at a minimum. Some experts advise up to eight cups a day to maintain good hydration.

CARPE DIEM:
Challenge yourself to drink more water. If you don't like the taste of plain water, flavor it with lemon or lime juice. Or take your favorite juice beverage and dilute it with half water.

10.

IF YOU SMOKE, QUIT

"I'm more proud of quitting smoking than of anything else I've done in my life, including winning an Oscar."

— Christine Lahti

- You know smoking isn't good for your health. Maybe you've tried to quit before but failed. Try again. Smoking is one of the hardest habits to break. Pick a good time to try to quit. If you've recently experienced a major loss in your life, now is not the time to try quitting.

- Heart disease, lung cancer, chronic bronchitis, cancer, and emphysema are all associated with smoking. Cancer of the mouth and throat can be caused by chewing tobacco.

- If you want to quit, the Smokefree.gov Online Quit Guide advises you to create a list of the reasons you want to quit and keeping that list in your purse, car, or jacket pocket—anywhere you normally keep cigarettes. You could put some of the health risks listed here on your list, but make it personal. The more it relates to you specifically, the better.

- Your doctor can write a prescription for medications to lessen the symptoms of quitting. Or try over-the-counter medications. Make a well-thought-out plan of how to quit and then set a quit date.

- Be sure to line up support for yourself during this difficult challenge. The best support people are often those who have quit smoking themselves. There are many online and telephone support services such as Quitline (1-800-QUIT-NOW) that can give you support.

CARPE DIEM:
If you smoke, make a plan for stopping and set a quit date today.

11.

GET THE WEIGHT OFF

"I'm the reason why I'm overweight. No one made me do it. I did it."
— Neil Cavuto

- As we age, it's easy to put on weight. That's because as we grow older our metabolism slows down. We simply don't need as much food as we used to. Unfortunately, our eating habits often don't change, and each year we add a few pounds—unless, of course, we make a conscious decision to eat less and exercise more.

- Take a minute to think about how you felt at your ideal weight. What words came up? Attractive? Fit? Capable? You can feel that way again. It doesn't matter if you are 10, 20, or even 30+ years older than that image in your head. Feeling healthy and having a good body image feels good, regardless of age. We recently watched a marathon and were so impressed to see a man in his 80s on the 20-mile line. Being fit and maintaining a healthy weight is within your means.

- Weight loss can lower blood pressure, reduce heart disease, reduce risk for diabetes and cancers, and lessen osteoarthritis symptoms. Even asthma and sleep apnea improve with weight loss.

- There's no secret to weight loss. It's simple: eat less, exercise more. Try these easy tips to get yourself rolling: never skip breakfast, reduce snacks between meals, lower your carbohydrate intake, eat less sugary/fatty foods, exercise daily, and don't eat after seven p.m. If the list is too overwhelming to take on all at once, pick one or two to implement over the next few weeks, then add another. Nothing will make you feel younger than being at your ideal weight.

CARPE DIEM:

It takes three weeks to form a new habit. Commit to one positive change to improve your health and lessen your weight and do it every day for the next three weeks.

12.

FIND SOLUTIONS TO SLEEP TROUBLES

"Sleep is the best meditation."
— Dalai Lama

- How's your sleep? Nothing is more essential for starting a day off well than getting a good night's sleep. Yet one in three people has trouble falling or staying asleep.

- Aging can affect sleep. As we grow older, our bodies make less important sleep hormones: melatonin and growth hormone. That's why you used to be able to sleep through anything and now awaken to the slightest noise. Or maybe you suffer from insomnia, due to aging or life stress. Menopause also causes sleep problems.

- Chronic illnesses also affect sleep. Your arthritis pain might be keeping you awake, or maybe your enlarged prostate forces you to get up several times to visit the bathroom. High blood pressure and heart disease might wake you during the night due to changes in your heart rate or breathing. Medication can affect sleep.

- Give yourself a fighting chance by improving your sleep habits:
  - Only use your bed for sleep and sex.
  - Don't watch TV in bed—it's too stimulating. Instead, try reading a book.
  - If stress is a factor, before heading to bed make a list of your worries and obligations then write a solution next to each.
  - Avoid alcohol. It makes you sleepy but also tends to make you wake up after falling asleep. Also avoid caffeine after noon.
  - If you wake up at night, don't look at the clock. If you don't fall back to sleep in 15 minutes, get up and quietly read until you feel sleepy again.

CARPE DIEM:

Get in the habit of going to bed at least eight hours before you need to get up. Remember, those who sleep well age slower and live longer.

13.

RESPECT THE PHYSICAL
SIGNS OF GRIEF

*"Among other things, Kathryn knew, grief
was physically exhausting."*
— Anita Shreve, *The Pilot's Wife*

- As you age, you experience loss. Maybe you have experienced the death of a loved one, or you've been diagnosed with a chronic or serious illness. Maybe your marriage has failed or your kids have grown, left, and rarely call.

- Grief feels bad physically. If you are grieving a loss, you might suffer from fatigue, headaches, stress, migraines, high blood pressure, and even body aches and pains.

- Grief can also cause exhaustion, uncontrollable crying, sleep disturbance, palpitations, shortness of breath, recurrent infections, high blood pressure, loss of appetite, stomach upsets, hair loss, and irritability.

- Preexisting painful problems such as arthritis may get worse, and other chronic problems often flare up as well. It's common for conditions that need careful control, like high blood pressure and diabetes, to be under less control during times of grief.

- These symptoms are telling you to slow down and turn inward to your grief. Take time to experience your loss—tell a good friend what you are feeling, attend a support group, or journal.

- Take care of your body. Breathe in and breathe out. Get lots of rest, eat healthy foods, drink plenty of fluids, and walk or exercise if you are up to it.

CARPE DIEM:
Right now, sit in a comfortable position. Take 10 deep,
slow breaths—filling and emptying your lungs completely.
Feel the calming effects throughout your body.

14.

COPE WITH A CHRONIC ILLNESS

"Take care of your body. It's the only place you have to live."
— Jim Rohn

• We often can't outrun our genes. Even if we do everything right to prevent a chronic illness we are genetically programmed for, thanks to our family history, it eventually tends to catch up with us.

• That's not to say we should give in and forego preventive methods—like maintaining a healthy, low-sugar diet with regular exercise to ward off diabetes—but we should also accept that some things we can't completely control. In other words, if you live with a chronic illness, don't fight it by denying it. Do whatever you can to learn how to manage it and regulate it, so it stays in the background and not the foreground of your life.

• Don't ignore your chronic illness. If you have high blood pressure, manage it well and you can stave off a stroke forever. The same goes with diabetes. Well-managed, it doesn't have to affect your longevity. If ignored, it can damage your nerves, eyes, kidneys, and more.

• To age gracefully and ensure you won't be debilitated by your illness in later years, learn all you can about it. Join a support group, attend health seminars, and see your doctor regularly. Don't let poor health insurance or finances get in your way. Many communities have programs to help people struggling with chronic illnesses get the medicine and care they need.

CARPE DIEM:
Which chronic illnesses are prevalent in your family of origin? Research preventive measures. If you already suffer from a chronic condition, seek out a new source of help or support today.

15.

MAKE FITNESS FUN

"You only get one body; it is the temple of your soul. Even God is willing to live there. If you truly treat your body like a temple, it will serve you well for decades. If you abuse it you must be prepared for poor health and a lack of energy."

— Ollie Hille

- Doing an activity you enjoy will not only help your physical body but add a sense of fun to your life—giving you a new zest and confidence as you grow older.

- What do you enjoy? Being outside? Take a hike or try mountain biking or mountain boarding. If that's too daring, how about cross-country skiing or a walk through the zoo? Always wanted to take ballroom or line-dancing lessons? Sign up! If you liked aerobics in the 80s, you'll love Zumba.

- Consider reading, listening to music, or watching TV while riding an exercise bike. Or put on your favorite tunes and walk fast through the neighborhood or dance in your living room.

- Vary your routine. You'll get less bored and also be less likely to get injured because you'll be keeping your muscles balanced. Walk one day, bicycle the next. Swim at the local pool one morning, rollerblade on the bike path the next.

- It is important to exercise consistently. If you like what you're doing, you'll stick to it. Besides, doing things you love keeps you feeling young.

CARPE DIEM:
Imagine things that bring you pleasure. How can you work exercise into this picture?

16.

LIFT WEIGHTS TO BOOST BODY AND BRAIN

"What we face may look insurmountable. But I learned something from all those years of training and competing. I learned something from all those sets and reps when I didn't think I could lift another ounce of weight. What I learned is that we are always stronger than we know."

— Arnold Schwarzenegger

- As we age, we naturally lose some brainpower. Things get harder to remember, complicated tasks become more challenging. But some of this can be countered by lifting weights regularly. A recent study had women ages 65 to 75 lift weights twice a week for a year. At the end, they were tested on their "executive functioning skills"—the ability to organize, make decisions, focus, and resolve conflicts. The women improved 10 to 12 percent from their original scores!

- As you age, your muscle fibers shrink, making them less sensitive to incoming messages from your nerves. This can affect your coordination, strength, and balance. Yet resistance exercise keeps your muscle fibers from shrinking and reverses this decline.

- Weight training also increases bone mass, lowering the risk of osteoporosis and fractures. Without regular weightlifting sessions, 50 percent of muscle mass is lost between the ages of 20 and 90 years.

- Aim for three 30-minute sessions a week. The goal is to be able to do two sets of 12 to 15 repetitions per exercise. Choose light enough weights to allow for this. You should not feel pain as you lift. Feeling some soreness the next day is normal, especially in the beginning.

CARPE DIEM:
Are you a member of a club, or do you have access to weights? A lot can be done with simple dumbbells. Figure a plan to begin, or maintain, a weight program today.

17.

TRY TAI CHI

*"Know yourself. Do your best. Make a little
progress everyday. Don't overdo it."*

— Master Jou Tsung Hwa

• Originally developed in China as a form of self-defense, tai chi
(pronounced "ty chee") is a graceful form of exercise that has
existed for some 2,000 years. Practiced regularly, tai chi can help
you reduce your stress and strengthen and nurture your body and
spirit. It is based on postures that get your good energy flowing
and helps you resist negative energy.

• It is often described as "meditation in motion" because it
promotes serenity through gentle movements, helping to connect
the mind and the body. When you are stressed by grief, aging, and
other demands, your energy becomes blocked and you feel tired,
depressed, and out of balance. The slow movements of tai chi
calm you, inviting harmony and peace into your body.

• Anyone can practice tai chi since it does not take physical prowess
and emphasizes technique over strength. Talk to your doctor if
you have joint, spine, or heart problems before starting a new
program.

• Tai chi has been shown to not only reduce stress but improve
flexibility and muscle strength, increase stamina and agility,
and heighten feelings of well-being. Other health benefits may
include reduced anxiety and depression, improved balance and
coordination, better sleep quality, lower blood pressure, and less
chronic pain.

CARPE DIEM:
If you are interested in tai chi, find a qualified
instructor in your area and sign up for a beginning
session. It's the perfect way to age gracefully.

18.

STAY YOUNG WITH YOGA

"Be infinitely flexible and constantly amazed."
— Jason Kravitz

• Yoga is an ancient form of exercise, over 3,000 years old. It originated in India and can promote both mental and physical health. Yoga strengthens you physically, emotionally, and spiritually. Many traditions acknowledge that being on a spiritual path is like being a warrior. Practicing yoga can help you become a peaceful warrior and inspire your capacity to deal with aging.

• Yoga has elements of ancient teachings that connect mind and body in an exercise form involving postures (asanas), breathing technique (pranayama), and meditation. The breathing techniques or purifications can enhance inner tranquility. Yoga teaches long, slow, deep breaths that help get oxygen to your cells and can help center you and remind you to nurture your spiritual life. Yogic breathing infuses your body with prana, or energy.

• Yoga can improve balance, flexibility, and strength. Proponents feel it even has an anti-aging effect and can improve concentration and endurance.

• Mentally, yoga has many positive effects including decreased anxiety and depressive symptoms, improving mood and memory, and helping people to feel more self-actualized and at ease with who they are.

• If you are new to yoga, start with a beginning class and an instructor who can individualize the techniques to your needs.

CARPE DIEM:
Check to see if any therapeutic yoga classes are available
in your area and if interested, try one today.

19.

GARDEN FOR YOUR BODY AND SOUL

"The best place to seek God is in a garden."
— George Bernard Shaw

• Gardening is therapeutic on many levels. It's satisfying to be outside smelling the earth and feeling the sun. It's spiritually satisfying to take part in helping things grow. It also feels good to get dirty and sweaty and eliminate the weeds of our lives as we dig away at the real ones in front of us. Don't be fooled. Gardening is not an "old person's" hobby—it is hard physical work and is one of the ancient arts of humankind.

• The regular exercise that you get from gardening has been shown to reduce the risk of heart disease and helps keep bodies flexible. Gardening cannot only build strength and cardiovascular fitness but can relieve stress and even provide nutritious food.

• Fruits and vegetables you grow yourself taste great and are better for you. Eating fresh-picked produce, versus produce that has traveled hundreds or thousands of miles to your grocery store, provides 100 percent of the nutrients it holds. In growing your own food, you also have control over the pesticides and fertilizers used. And growing fresh herbs can add some spice to your life.

• Working in a garden connects you with nature and the rhythms of life. You must slow down and live in "garden time."

CARPE DIEM:
Plan a small garden that you'll plant this spring. If it's winter, create an indoor garden with a few pots and seeds.

20.

WALK EVERY DAY

"My grandmother started walking five miles a day when she was 60. She's 97 now, and we don't know where the hell she is."
— Ellen DeGeneres

- Our community is full of daily walkers. One woman in particular stands out—Sophia. Sophia is 92 years old and incredibly sharp and spry. She walks a one-mile loop two to three times a day. She does it for her physical health, but along the way she also makes many friends, including all the dogs to whom she hands out biscuits. She inspires us to no end.

- Walking is great for any age, but as people grow older, they tend to walk more. It's easy on the bones and joints and offers a peaceful break each day. Have you ever noticed that you always feel better when you return from a walk than when you left? It's a time for reflection and calm as well as exercise.

- I (Kirby) often "prescribe" walking for my patients. Just 10 minutes of exercise four or five times a day acts like a medication in the way it lowers blood pressure. New federal exercise guidelines suggest that several short bouts of exercise are just as good for you as one longer work-out a day.

CARPE DIEM:

Get in the habit of a daily walk, even if it is just once or twice around the block. Use it to unwind after work or to get your body and heart moving in the morning.

Caring for Yourself Intellectually As You Age

"I still have a full deck; I just shuffle slower now."
— Author Unknown

As our brains age, it may take us longer to learn new information, and we may not be able to think as quickly or sharply. We may have a harder time with tip-of-the-tongue recall of certain words and names. We might be more easily distracted and be less capable of multitasking.

But scientists also believe that older brains have unique strengths. They now know that our brains keep making new neurons even into our 70s. And older people seem to be better at what is called the "human-centered design process"—innovative creating that involves empathizing, defining, ideating, prototyping, and testing. We're also better at complex reasoning.

The bottom line is that the aging brain is far more capable and resilient than we used to think.

So keep your mind active, and stay confident about your cognitive abilities. Just because you can't find your car keys doesn't mean you don't have profound wisdom and intellectual powers to share.

21.

PAMPER YOUR BRAIN

"Great minds discuss ideas; average minds discuss events; small minds discuss people."
— Eleanor Roosevelt

- You may have bellyached over your saggy bottom, cursed your crow's feet, lamented about your love handles, and gone to great lengths to hide your graying hair. But when was the last time you gave any serious thought to your brain health?

- There are simple ways to improve your brain function as you age. First, take care of your heart with a heart-healthy lifestyle. Everything that is good for your heart is also good for your brain.

- Don't smoke. It's a risk factor for both heart disease and stroke and may increase the risk of Alzheimer's.

- Exercise. It's important to be physically active throughout life. It can improve the ability of the brain.

- Keep your mind active with brain games and social engagements.

- Finally, relax. Don't fret excessively if you feel like your brain is slowing down. Accept that memory loss is a normal part of aging, just like creaky knees. You remember the important things in life. Don't sweat the details.

CARPE DIEM:
Make a list of all the activities you enjoy (or would like to try) that exercise your brain. Do one of them today.

22.

RECOGNIZE NORMAL MEMORY LOSS WITH AGING

*"I think you remember everything…you just
can't bring it to mind all the time."*

— Edward Albee

• Like everything physical, our brain slows as we age.

• You forget something and you worry—is it Alzheimer's? Normal age-related memory loss means having a harder time recalling new information—like a person's name that you met recently or the name of a book you finished a few months ago. It can also mean forgetting where you put your keys, where you parked, or a friend's birthday. Also, you might not recall information or complete cognitive tasks as quickly as before.

• Normal memory loss doesn't impact your ability to live a full and productive life, though. You simply may need to be more conscious of where you put things or make more lists to remember tasks.

• If memory loss crosses the line to being uncertain if you had lunch, forgetting the route home, not remembering a recent get-together, or forgetting to put shoes on when you leave the house, it's time for an evaluation.

• If you feel you have experienced memory loss more recently, see your doctor. There are other, reversible causes of memory loss besides dementia. They include stress, poor sleep, medications, head trauma, depression, alcoholism (and mixing alcohol with certain medicines), a vitamin B-12 deficiency, tumors, and hypothyroidism.

CARPE DIEM:
Are you forgetting little things? Try not to worry
about normal age-related memory loss.

23.

KNOW THE SIGNS OF ALZHEIMER'S OR DEMENTIA

"You're so beautiful," said Alice. "I'm afraid of looking at you and not knowing who you are."
"I think that even if you don't know who I am someday, you'll still know that I love you."
"What if I see you, and I don't know that you're my daughter, and I don't know that you love me?"
"Then, I'll tell you that I do, and you'll believe me."
— Lisa Genova, *Still Alice*

- Sometimes, differences can be subtle between normal age-related memory loss and Alzheimer's or dementia. That's because memory loss is a sign of dementia, but there are many others. According to the Mayo Clinic, these include:

  - Taking longer to complete familiar tasks, such as following a known recipe
  - Asking the same questions over and over again
  - Mixing words up—saying "bed" instead of "table," for example
  - Misplacing items in strange places, like putting milk in a cupboard
  - Getting lost while walking or driving around a familiar place
  - Undergoing sudden changes in behavior or mood
  - Finding it harder to follow directions

- If you have concerns for you or your spouse or friend, see a doctor. Don't fall into the trap of thinking there's nothing to do about it. While a hard and fast solution is yet to be discovered, there are medicines that slow memory loss in some dementia patients, and new ones are always being explored.

CARPE DIEM:
Do you ever forget where you are or how to get home? If so, call your doctor for a memory-loss evaluation.

24.

FEED YOUR BRAIN

*"The mind is like an iceberg. It floats with one-
seventh of its bulk above water."*

— Sigmund Freud

• With Baby Boomers aging, more and more products are coming to
market to solve aging woes. Some even claim to increase brain power.
What's real?

• These studied nutrients are thought to feed the brain and increase its
functioning. They include:

- Folic acid. Make sure you are getting enough of this necessary
nutrient each day by eating plenty of leafy greens, broccoli,
beans, citrus fruits, avocados, okra, seeds, nuts, and fortified
breads. The daily recommend dose is 400 micrograms.

- Choline. Choline is thought to enhance memory in
Alzheimer's patients. Dr. Andrew Weil suggests 500 mg. of
this micronutrient, which also supports the liver. Choline
is naturally found in eggs, beef, soy, salmon, peanut butter,
broccoli, and Brussels sprouts.

- Ginkgo biloba. Taken daily, this herb has been found by the
Mayo Clinic to improve memory in some people, especially
those with certain types of dementia. Take 80 to 240 mg daily.

- Omega-3 fatty acids. Our brains need healthy fats to function
well. University of Maryland studies have shown omega-3s
increase brain performance and memory. Take up to 1400 mg
of DHA (fish oil) per day to see benefits.

- Phosphatidylserine (PS). Used commonly in Europe, this
compound supports neurotransmitters and aids memory,
reasoning, and concentration.

CARPE DIEM:
Check with your doctor about taking these or other brain-
enhancing nutrients in amounts that are right for you.

25.

CLEAR YOUR MIND

"I deepen my experience of God through prayer, meditation, and forgiveness."

— Marianne Williamson

- It's important at any age to take mental breaks. A basic meditation technique that can help you relax is "clearing your mind." Stop what you are doing and close your eyes. Concentrate on one pleasant thought, word, or image and let the rest of your worries slip way. Begin to breathe slowly and deeply, monitoring the deep breaths with a hand on your stomach.

- If other thoughts should enter your mind, don't be discouraged. Just relax, breathe deeply, and try again.

- Reduce distractions, noise, and interruptions as much as possible. Sit comfortably, loosen any tight clothing, kick off your shoes, and relax your muscles.

- Spend several minutes with your mind focused on this peaceful sensation and your body will naturally relax as well. With practice, clearing your mind can help you feel refreshed, more energetic, and better able to tackle the next task at hand.

CARPE DIEM:
Set aside 10 minutes daily to practice clearing your mind.

26.

CHANNEL YOUR ENERGIES

*"Concentration comes out of a combination
of confidence and hunger."*
— Arnold Palmer

- It is easy to get caught up in today's frantic pace, feeling as if your energies are going in multiple directions. Multitasking is one thing, but with the speed of modern life, it can feel more like "multiliving."

- To cognitively deal well with aging, be more single-minded. Focus on those activities that are important in your life, and channel your energies in those directions. For example, if you are active in the community, decide which organization's purpose is most important to you and give your time to it. Let most of the others go.

- Define which activities give your life meaning and which feel more like obligations. If you'd rather take your grandchild fishing or hiking, do that instead of attending an obligatory social meeting.

- Channel your energy more toward your desires than your "shoulds" to experience a peaceful, uncluttered mind.

CARPE DIEM:
Where do you want to focus your energies? Make a list of the top five. Are you finding time to touch these activities almost every day?

27.

BE A LIFELONG LEARNER

*"The voyage of discovery is not in seeking new
landscapes but in having new eyes."*
— Marcel Proust

• Remember how exciting it was to be a student? It's important
for people of all ages, especially those in later years, to learn
new things. People need to keep learning after school ends and
continue solving intellectual and mental tasks after they stop
working.

• Stop and consider which subjects you're interested in but never
had a chance to study. Think back to your high school or college
days. Which classes seemed exciting or which careers did you
consider yet forego? Astronomy? Art? Anatomy?

• Learn whatever you can about one of your subjects of interest.
Audit a class at a university. Take a course offered through your
city, county, senior center, or extension office. Visit with a friend
or colleague who pursued a career in this area of study.

• When you are done with the first subject, try another. Make
learning a lifelong habit.

CARPE DIEM:
Visit your local library and browse the
shelves. See what sparks your interest.

28.

LEARN A NEW SKILL

"We must always change, renew, rejuvenate
ourselves, otherwise we harden."

— Johann Wolfgang von Goethe

- A great way to exercise your brain is to learn a new skill or task. For ideas, just look around your house or apartment. Certainly there is something that needs repair or fixing—new brakes for your bike, a landscaping project, or a leaky faucet.

- Or, learn a new skill that challenges both body and brain, like racquetball or a new dance step. Or play a videogame with your grandchild, such as Wii bowling or Guitar Hero, where you play the drums or sing to a broadcasted tune.

- Tasks with several steps to complete challenge your brain the most. That's because they exercise your executive functioning skills (planning, organization, and multitasking), which decline as people age, usually starting at age 70. If it's appealing, challenge yourself with a larger project or task, such as researching your genealogy or writing a collection of your life experiences.

- And remember—Rome wasn't built in a day and neither will your new skill be. To learn something complex takes time and repetition. And it is this very time and repetition that will enhance your cognitive function.

CARPE DIEM:
Which skill would you like to learn? Think about what you've
seen others do that you wish you could do and try that.

29.

PLAY A GAME

"Games lubricate the body and the mind."
— Benjamin Franklin

- There's a reason older people often enjoy playing cards and doing crossword puzzles. They are mentally challenging games that often demand strategy.

- Do you have a group of friends to play bridge, poker, or Bunco with? How about a friend who loves Scrabble as much as you do? Or grandkids who enjoy board games? If so, schedule a regular date! If not, locate a club through your neighborhood, city, place of worship, or senior center.

- Also consider playing solitary games to keep your mind sharp. Jigsaw puzzles, crossword puzzles, Sudoku, and solitaire itself work well!

- Strengthen brainpower by playing interactive games online. In your Internet search tool, type in "games to increase brain power" and hundreds of sites will pop up. Try the games offered by AARP (www.aarp.org/health/brain-health/brain_games).

- Be skeptical about spending money on cognitive programs. You don't have to invest in expensive brain games to see benefits.

CARPE DIEM:
Which games do you enjoy playing? Make a goal to play that game today or set up a session with a friend or group for next week.

30.

JOIN A BOOK CLUB

"The more that you read, the more things you will know.
The more that you learn, the more places you'll go."
— Dr. Seuss

- Reading feeds not only your brain but your soul and emotions as well.

- There are a lot of options for joining book clubs these days besides friends spontaneously getting together and starting a club. Local libraries organize clubs, as do retail bookstores, places of worship, and senior centers. You can even join a book club online.

- Don't let failing eyesight keep you away from books. Check out your library's section of books in large print, or consider an electronic reader where you can make the font larger. And carry those reading glasses with you!

- If you've retired but would like to keep up with happenings in your field, subscribe to industry journals. If you've started a new hobby, say photography or organic gardening, subscribe to magazines for tips and tricks.

- Maybe it's time to explore a new genre. If all you've ever read is literary novels, how about trying a romance novel or a Western? Or maybe an autobiography or biography on someone you admire or are curious about? Historical fiction is also a fun option— giving you a story and a realistic taste of life in a past era.

CARPE DIEM:
Visit a bookstore in person or online and search
"top 100 books" or "best book club books" and
select one to read on your own or with others.

31.

TRY A NEW RECIPE, TAKE A NEW ROUTE

"When in doubt, make a fool of yourself. There is a microscopically thin line between being brilliantly creative and acting like the most gigantic idiot on earth. So what the hell, leap."
—Cynthia Heimel

- Humans are creatures of habit. We like the predictable, but routines can leave us feeling unchallenged and bored. Changing up our routines helps keep our thinking sharp and our brains young.

- Are you stuck in a rut when it comes to meals? Do you always buy the same items at the grocery store? Shake up your routine. Find a new recipe in a magazine or the newspaper and give it a try. You'll not only change up your routine but you might introduce new foods into your diet as well.

- Do you always drive the same route home or to your favorite store? Try a different way now and then—a known trick to combat age-related memory loss. Do you resist driving in the city or at night? Or do you always let your husband or wife drive? If your driving and vision skills are still strong and your reluctance is more about habit, take the wheel.

CARPE DIEM
In what small ways can you shake up your routine today?

32.

EXERCISE TO STAY QUICK-WITTED

"Exercise doesn't make you smarter…it just makes you normal."
— John Medina

- When we exercise our bodies, we exercise our brains. When we move, our brains send numerous messages to our bodies, even during simple physical tasks like bike riding.

- A study at the University of Pittsburgh recently showed that regular exercise improves blood flow to the brain and speeds learning.

- Dr. John Ratey at Harvard states that regular exercise increases metabolism, improves attention and mood, and decreases stress, which make the brains work better. Through studies, he's found that with regular exercise, "Brain cells actually become more resilient and pliable and more ready to link up, [allowing] us to retain new information."

- A study published recently in the Annals of Internal Medicine also found that older people who exercise three times a week or more lowered their chances of developing Alzheimer's or other dementias by one-third over those who didn't.

- These are sound reasons to establish an exercise plan and stick to it!

CARPE DIEM:
Do you exercise at least 30 minutes, three times a week? If yes, be sure to get in your 30 minutes today. If not, start today with a 5- or 10-minute walk.

33.

KEEP UP WITH CURRENT EVENTS

"A newspaper is the center of a community, it's one
of the tent poles of the community, and that's not
going to be replaced by websites and blogs."
— Michael Connelly

• A great way to keep cognitively healthy as you age is to stay informed on current events. Read the newspaper and news magazines, and watch the news.

• If you are stuck on one newspaper or one news channel, shake up your routine by watching a different one. For example, tune in to the BBC news on your radio (or stream it online). If you read Time, try Newsweek. If you get your local city's newspaper, try the New York Times or Washington Post.

• Many newspapers today offer an online subscription. Even when you just order the Sunday paper, you often get the online subscription all week for free.

• In your local paper, don't skip the editorial section. It's a good way to keep a pulse on your community.

CARPE DIEM:
Check out a novel news source today.

34.

BEFRIEND TECHNOLOGY

"One day soon the Gillette company will announce the development
of a razor that, thanks to a computer microchip, can actually travel
ahead in time and shave beard hairs that don't even exist yet."
— Dave Barry

- In these fast times of changing technology, it's hard for anyone of any age to keep up.

- Older people who didn't use technology much in their careers or whose career days are long past often have a hard time with technology. The change is like leaping an ocean rather than a stream.

- Instead of feeling embarrassed or befuddled by new technology, get help in learning at least the basics. Access to the internet is like having the best libraries in the world at your fingertips. Take an "introduction to technology" class at your library or senior center, or ask a younger family member for help.

- Besides providing information, the internet and devices like smart phones and tablets connect you to the world socially via email, texting, Twitter, Skype, and Facebook. How nice it is to visit face-to-face with far-away family members via video conferencing or to text or post quick thoughts or photos to friends. It makes the world a smaller place and helps you feel more connected.

- One caveat: try to get your information from reputable sources online. If you go to a trusted source, you won't run the risk of being fed false or unsubstantiated information.

CARPE DIEM:
Is there a technology skill you'd like to learn?
Who can you ask for help today?

35.

PICK UP AN INSTRUMENT

"Music does not excite until it is performed."
— Benjamin Britten

• Music is a great way to exercise your brain, whether it's listening or playing.

• Researchers at Stanford University have shown that musical training improves how the brain processes language.

• Did you play an instrument in the past? If it's collecting dust in a closet, pull it out. Play a tune or strum some bars. If your interest is piqued, continue playing or take a few refresher lessons.

• If you are experiencing some memory loss or early dementia, music is a great way to stimulate memories. A friend who works with the elderly shared a story of an Alzheimer's patient who was encouraged to play the piano. She started playing songs from her childhood, even though she often had trouble remembering where she was. Dementia patients who lose their ability to talk can often sing.

• If you never played an instrument, feed your creative brain by attending a concert or seeing a performance or play. Better yet, learn to play a new instrument or join a choir. If those options seem out of reach, simply sing along as you drive around town!

CARPE DIEM:
What are some ways you can bring music into your life beyond what you currently do? Explore at least one option today.

36.

GO BACK TO YOUR ROOTS

*"To understand where you are going, you must
understand where you come from."*
— Celtic Proverb

- One of the great things about being older is having a past. You have a history of people, places, and things that have been dear to you and have brought meaning to your life.

- Rewind your life. Spool through your memories. See it like segments of a movie. Relive some of the highlights. Recall some of the characters who have traveled with you. See how far you have traveled. If you'd like, literally sit down and watch old family movies or sift through boxes of photos, letters, scrapbooks, yearbooks, and personal writings and journals.

- You have come a long way. You have had wonderful experiences. You have survived difficulties and loss. You know that life changes and nothing stays the same.

- As you look back, think about themes in your life. What have you always enjoyed? Who have you always loved? This is your life story. Cherish it.

CARPE DIEM:
What are some of your most cherished life experiences?
Write at least one of them down today.

37.

LIVE MINDFULLY

"Be moderate in order to taste the joys of life in abundance."
— Epicurus

- As we age, we grow into ourselves. We know when we are feeling centered and when we are off kilter. Little signs, like feeling irritable or unsatisfied, tell us when we are out of touch with ourselves or some need. Recognizing these signs benefits us greatly.

- Once you become aware of being off balance you can act to realign yourself.

- One way to do so is to live mindfully—consciously choosing to focus your thoughts on things that bring beauty and goodness to you and others. When you are mindful, you watch the thoughts that run through your brain and choose which ones to follow.

- Mindful living also means surrounding yourself with people and activities that bring you meaning, rather than seeking satisfaction in less healthy ways. It means recognizing when you slip into a bad habit or destructive train of thought, and stopping it.

- Ultimately, mindful living is about choice—choosing to lead your life, rather than allowing your life to lead you. It almost guarantees that you will act with integrity and authenticity as you move through your life. The reward? A rich, satisfying, and meaningful life.

CARPE DIEM:
What thoughts are running through your head today? Be a bystander and simply observe, without judgment. Then gently redirect yourself in a more positive direction, if needed.

38.

ALLAY YOUR FINANCIAL CONCERNS AND FEARS FOR THE FUTURE

"Money is neither my God nor my devil."
— Dan Millman

- As you age, you may be worrying about finances. Do you have enough to retire? What if a major medical problem saps your resources? Will you need long-term care? Finances are a concern no matter what level of financial resources you possess. That's because the future is unknown.

- Take stock of your resources. If you do not have a financial planner, get one. Knowing your net worth and the projected cost of living during retirement is important. Make a plan and stick to it as best you can.

- Will you eventually need long-term care? Almost 70 percent of people over age 65 do. A great resource to figure costs and see options in your area is the National Clearinghouse for Long Term Care at www.longtermcare.gov.

- Most states have a Department on Aging and resources for Eldercare. For example, if you visit the national Eldercare locator at www.eldercare.gov, you can search for various resources in your area on topics from Alzheimer's care and financial assistance to health insurance and housing options.

- It's important to have good medical coverage. The number one cause of bankruptcy in the U.S. is catastrophic medical problems.

- Also get your will, living will, and advance directives in order.

CARPE DIEM:
Take stock of your financial situation and consider all possible future needs. No one plans on the worst, but it can happen anyway. It's a lot to look at all at once, so pick one area of financial or future planning and start tackling it today.

39.

TAKE CONTROL OF YOUR TIME

*"Time is free, but it's priceless. You can't own it, but
you can use it. You can't keep it, but you can spend it.
Once you've lost it you can never get it back."*

— Harvey MacKay

• It may seem like time is whizzing by at an accelerated pace as
you age, but there is always time to do what you deem important
and meaningful in life. Do you feel in control of how your most
precious resource, your time here on earth, is used?

• Choose how you want to spend your time. Think twice before
saying yes to things you feel you should or must do, despite the
fact that they don't really interest you. Block out time on your
calendar and do things that matter to you. Schedule time for
working out and walks with friends as if they are just as important
as your work or social meetings.

• What are your passions? Activities that make you lose track of
time? Do more of those. Who interests you? Spend more time
with those people.

• When people retire, their worlds open up and they get to choose
how to fill their days. Some people enter this without much
thought, getting lost in a wide-open schedule. Others know
precisely how they want to fill their time.

• Time, like money, is a precious resource. Spend it wisely.

CARPE DIEM:
Look back on the last week. How did you spend
your time? What, if anything, was missing from your
days? Dedicate some time to that activity today.

40.

KEEP A GRATITUDE JOURNAL

*"It is the sweet, simple things in life which
are the real ones after all."*

— Laura Ingalls Wilder

- Want the key to happiness? Be grateful. Feel lucky. Appreciate the little joys of life.

- Remind yourself of what you are grateful for and what's going well in your life by keeping a gratitude journal. Write down everything, big and small. Is it your granddaughter's smile? Sharing a joke with a friend? The way the light sifts through your window in the morning hours?

- Gratitude journals can be an extremely powerful way to stay focused on the positive and reduce the negative in your life. They get you in the habit of focusing on what's right in your life versus what needs improvement. They let you see your "house" as complete rather than in repair or needing work.

- Consider this: You are what you think. If you think about how lucky you are to own this house, have this family, live in this area, enjoy these hobbies, have these friends, sit on this couch, etc., you are going to feel lucky. And grateful. Writing it down gives it extra sticking power.

- Grateful people are happier, healthier, less stressed, and more fulfilled. And they take less for granted.

CARPE DIEM:

Get a notebook and write "Gratitude Journal" on the
front. Before bed, write down five or more things that
you are grateful for, or list positive things that happened
during the day. You'll feel better and sleep better, too!

EMBRACING THE EMOTIONS OF AGING

*"The best and most beautiful things in the
world cannot be seen or even touched.*

They must be felt with the heart."

— Helen Keller

Your emotions are trying to teach you something.

We believe that your emotions are the tool your soul uses to get your attention. "I'm going to make your mind and body feel this certain way to express my truth," it says.

Your feelings about aging are not good or bad, right or wrong. They simply are. And whether you are feeling happy, angry, sad, anxious, regretful, fearful, numb, or any other emotion, your feelings are simply trying to get your attention.

I'm here for a reason, they say. *Witness me. Embrace me. Express me.*

And in return I will move you in the direction of your best life.

41.

LEAN INTO AGING

"Serenity is not freedom from the storm, but peace amid the storm."
— Anonymous

- A lot of emotions go along with growing older. Most of us feel mixed—at times happy and satisfied and at other times regretful and sad. It's important to honor all of your feelings as you age. Just because you are older doesn't mean you've got it all figured out and therefore won't have to deal with many feelings. We are human until the day we die, and humans are emotional creatures.

- When it comes to hard feelings, do the opposite of what everyone tells you to do—in other words, lean into what you are feeling rather than ignoring it or turning away. This method is far more effective, and in some ways more interesting. It opens you to growth and change—another constant with humans until the day we die.

- Karen Horney, an early 20th century psychoanalyst, describes three responses to stress: Some people move away from it; some move against the source of the stress; and a third group moves toward it. But there is a fourth option: Simply leaning into the emotion as you would a strong wind or current.

- Leaning into aging means not moving against the current, but walking gracefully with it, at your own pace. You don't let aging overtake you and steer you like a bumping log. Rather, you flow with it purposefully.

CARPE DIEM:
List the ways you have moved against aging, the ways you have withdrawn from aging, and the ways you have played victim to it.

42.

GRIEVE AND MOURN YOUR LOSSES

"Deposits of unfinished grief reside in more hearts
that I ever imagined. Until these pockets are opened
and their contents aired openly, they block unimagined
amounts of human growth and potential."
— Robert Kavanaugh

- Life doesn't happen without losses, and as we age, they seem to accumulate. People we love die, friendships we once cherished dissolve, careers we thought would flourish fizzle. It's easy to focus on these losses and get stuck in regret, saying, "I haven't done enough with my life."

- If you are feeling stuck, it's time to grieve. By grieving and mourning your losses—looking them straight in the eye, feeling their hurt and pain, and when you are ready, reconciling yourself to them—you will find the lightness to move forward and achieve new dreams and goals.

- Grief is usually associated with death, but it applies to all losses in life. We grieve when we lose something of value. Recognize your grief over the slow loss of your life as you have known it.

- With grief comes a wide range of emotions. Shock, numbness, denial, confusion, anxiety, guilt, and regret are common. You might also feel anger, blame, resentment, and sadness. These feelings can be all-consuming and can make you feel you are losing your way in your life—yet they are normal and necessary emotions.

- It's necessary to dose yourself with your grief. But in general you should feel that you're moving toward your grief while affirming your need to mourn.

CARPE DIEM:
Do a quiet activity that allows you to reflect on your life. Instead of keeping busy and speeding up, slow down. Let feelings come up.

43.

FORGIVE YOURSELF AND OTHERS

*"Forgiveness is a 'selective remembering'—a conscious
decision to focus on love and let the rest go."*
— Marianne Williamson

- All of us have regrets. It's hard to live a life without any. Maybe there are some past actions, words, or decisions you made that you are not proud of and wish you could take back. Or, maybe they were inactions—opportunities you let pass due to fear or circumstance. Possibly it's something someone did to you.

- Sometimes people have a hard time releasing big regrets and moving on. Instead, they pine for what could have been, getting stuck in the land of "woulda, coulda, shoulda" and the far-off planet of "if only."

- Regrets and grudges are like a leash—they keep you tied to the past. It's time to forgive yourself, and others, for past regrets and mistakes. Forgiveness sets you free from guilt and blame and lets you move forward toward serenity.

- The first step toward forgiveness is acceptance. Okay, it happened. Maybe not the way you hoped, but it is what it is. Trust yourself that you made the best decision you could in the moment. Trust that you didn't act with malice, more likely with fear or confusion—as did others who may have hurt you.

- Hold an image of you in that time and surround yourself with love and peace. Reframe it, redefine it. And replace it with an image of being free from that leash—of what can be, not what wasn't.

CARPE DIEM:
Fill in this blank: "If only I would have _____, my
life would have been better." Over the coming weeks,
consciously work toward releasing this regret.

44.

OPEN TO YOUR FEELINGS

"Be true to yourself and to your feelings. Those are the
only things in your life that will never lie to you."

— Anonymous

• What are you feeling these days? What do you feel when you
consider how much time has passed, and what the future holds?
Aging—and the changes that go along with it—can bring on a
mixture of feelings.

• Open to your feelings—all of them. Remember, they are not right
or wrong, they simply are. Allow yourself to feel whatever it is
you are feeling without judging yourself. Share your feelings with a
trusted friend or family member, or write them down in a journal.

• Try not to look for quick fixes—buying new clothes, trying new
products, moving to a new house, taking an expensive vacation—
or assume that making a change will solve things. Quick
conclusions may increase your feelings of despair and resistance
toward aging.

• The only thing that truly helps emotions is to shine the gentle light
of awareness onto them. Get to know your feelings about aging
like they are sad and lonely friends. Hold them to you for comfort.

• Likewise, bask in your feelings of satisfaction and joy. Collect your
happy memories and put them in your back pocket—feel them
there as you walk forward in your life.

CARPE DIEM:

Using old magazines, make a "feelings collage." Clip images that
capture the many feelings you've been having lately and paste
them onto poster board. Share it with someone you trust.

45.

ACKNOWLEDGE YOUR
FEAR OF DYING

*"I'm not afraid of dying; I just don't want
to be there when it happens."*
— Woody Allen

- In part, aging is scary because each year brings us closer to the end of life.

- Death is The Big Unknown. And all unknowns are scary—especially this one, which means leaving everything we know and everyone we love.

- Life seemed vast and nearly endless when we were young. We had plenty of time to do everything we wanted to do. Now, time seems to go by much more quickly. The days, weeks, and months seem to flash by. There's a sense of desperation to hold on to every moment, every memory and feeling.

- If you have experienced the death of people you love, death is closer to you. Or, if you have endured cancer or other dark diagnoses, you've faced death. These experiences might give you a sense that you are vulnerable and simply marching toward death. Try to shift your focus toward life today and what brings you joy and meaning.

- If the thought of dying grips you with fear, try to get in touch with the circle of life—birth/life/death—and see it as normal. If you are religious, rely on your faith. You are not disappearing; you will have an afterlife. Take comfort in knowing you will be remembered.

CARPE DIEM:
One of the best responses to a fear of death is to vow to live fully. If there are things you have wanted to do but never got around to them—do them now. Today, make your bucket list.

46.

KNOW THE SIGNS OF DEPRESSION

"We must embrace pain and burn it as fuel for our journey."
— Kenji Miyazawa

- Depression is far too common among older people. It can be a consequence of enduring loss without mourning. Feeling down or blue occasionally is normal—and often a symptom that we have some emotional business that needs our attention.

- If feeling down gets worse instead of better over a few weeks and you have other mood symptoms as well (anger, hopelessness, irritability, etc.), then you may want to see a physician or mental health caregiver for an evaluation.

- Symptoms of depression include:
    - Little interest in things that normally give pleasure
    - Feeling down or depressed most of the time
    - Trouble falling asleep or staying asleep
      No energy and being tired most of the time
    - A change in appetite (usually a decreased appetite, although some people react to stress by eating more)
    - Feeling like a failure or having feelings of guilt for no good reason
    - Having trouble concentrating or thinking clearly
    - Moving slowly or being fidgety
    - Feeling hopeless or thinking about suicide
    - Losing touch with friends

CARPE DIEM:
Do you have more than a few of these symptoms? Make an appointment with a mental health caregiver today.

47.

LIST YOUR SURVIVAL STRATEGIES

*"To live is to suffer; to survive is to find
some meaning in the suffering."*
— Friedrich Nietzsche

• If you've recently experienced a major loss or are feeling depressed, it's time to tap into your survival strategies.

• What has helped you cope with stress and loss in the past? These strategies will probably help now and into the future as well.

• Make a list of the most difficult times in your life and the ways in which you helped yourself live through them. Did you spend time with family? Turn to your faith? Meet regularly with a friend? Spend time in nature? See a counselor or attend a group? Help take care of someone else?

• Can you make use of any of these survival techniques today?

• Knowing what calms you is also important. What brings you peace and comfort? Getting a massage? Taking a walk? Going for a swim? Talking to your sister? Walking the dog? Meditating? Consider what works for you, or explore something new that seems appealing and satisfying.

CARPE DIEM:
If you are struggling, make a list of what you need to
do to get through the next month. Ask your friends
and family to help you meet these needs.

48.

SOOTHE YOUR STRESS

*"Tension is who you think you should
be. Relaxation is who you are."*

— Chinese Proverb

- Do you feel stressed? Uptight? Can't keep up with everything anymore? The feelings that come with getting older can be overwhelming and cause stress, as can natural memory loss and sleep issues that sometimes accompany aging.

- The first step in dealing with stress is to identify the sources. Have you experienced a major life event, such as moving, your kids leaving home, death of someone close to you, or an illness or accident? If you have, know that you need some downtime to recover.

- Daily pressure to get more done than you have time for also causes stress. Carrying stress affects your physical health. When stressed, your body is in a constant flight or fight state, which throws your adrenal hormones out of sync. The result is constant exhaustion.

- How do you respond to stress? Observe how you react under stress—do you curse other drivers or get upset over little mishaps? These are clues that you are out of balance and need to go out and enjoy yourself or do a calming activity.

- To relieve stress, work in periods of mental and physical relaxation throughout the day. When you take time to relax, you restore the balance between mind, body, and spirit. It's like taking a dip in a cool pool and coming out refreshed.

CARPE DIEM:

Make a list of the stressors that are in your life. Reflect on ways to calm yourself. For example, choose a single word, such as security, peace, or love. Contemplate the meaning of the word you have selected. Focus on this word as you see it in your mind's eye.

49.

TRUST YOUR TRUE GRIT

"Life is like photography. You use the negative to develop."
— Anonymous

- One benefit of having lived a while is learning how to get through rough times. Everyone experiences troubles in their lives, and there is some truth to the idea of "what doesn't kill you makes you stronger." Our reward? Calm in the face of danger, and a knowing that life has its ups and downs. Endure the down and an up is likely around the corner.

- As you've grown older, you've learned some things. In other words, you've matured. You know who you are. You know your strengths and weaknesses. So what if you never become great at sales or a dynamic public speaker. Who cares? You've released what you can't do and concentrated on what you can.

- Your life experiences have made you resilient, and you've got coping skills.

- With that in mind, trust that you can face the challenges of aging. You've endured pain, loss, and hardship before. If your future holds some challenges, know that you'll be able to address them as they arise. This doesn't mean going it alone. Quite the opposite. It means allowing yourself to be human, asking for help, tapping into your strengths, having faith, and keeping going. Trust your true grit.

CARPE DIEM:
What are some truths and lessons you've learned through life? Share one with a younger person today by having a conversation or writing and sending an e-mail or card.

50.

FIND PLEASURE EACH DAY

"Pleasure is nature's test, her sign of approval. When man is happy, he is in harmony with himself and his environment."
— Oscar Wilde

- When it comes right down to it, nothing matters more in life than joy—receiving it and giving it—and being with the ones you love. Call a beloved friend, daughter, son, grandchild, or relative today and plan a fun, meaningful outing or adventure.

- If you are looking toward retirement, you might be wondering how you will fill your days. You probably can't wait to travel, get to the garden, or simply read. But retirement often means a loss of social interaction and a sense of self-worth—especially if you've poured yourself into your career. It will demand a new schedule and a new set of priorities.

- Make a list of activities that bring you pleasure. Write down old favorites and new ideas too. Also, think about what you long for in life—is it more time in nature? Intellectual stimulation? Closeness with friends and family? Put these on your list, too.

- If a loved one has recently died, you might think that having fun dishonors the loss. To the contrary, the person who died would relish in seeing you enjoy life.

- Don't worry about being self-indulgent. Some traditional mindsets promote that pleasure is downright evil or a waste of time. Others see value in only working and producing. Shed these old ideas and allow yourself pleasure each and every day.

CARPE DIEM:

What's on tap for today? Plan on doing something you enjoy, no matter how hectic your schedule. Spending time with friends can be one of the very best ways to support your well-being. Make a date to have lunch with friend you enjoy being around.

51.

SHAKE UP YOUR ROUTINES

"The less routine the more life."
— Amos Bronson Alcott

- Do you find that with each passing year, you get more invested in your routine? You read the paper each morning, and if you don't get to it your day seems off-kilter. The neighbors can set their clock to your dog walk each day.

- Many people prefer a protected, climate-controlled life devoted to minimizing risks. Routines bring comfort; that's why we fall into them. Life is predictable. We know what's next, and we are ready for it.

- Yet routines can be stifling. More than mere daily habits, they can become a way of life, and anything outside that way of life seems wrong or annoying. Routines can even roll over into our thoughts and beliefs. Productivity and sense of meaning can drop when you become mentally and physically dulled from doing the same things over and over.

- If you hear yourself saying, "That's just the way it is" or feel uncomfortable with people who don't live or look like you do, it's time to shake up your routine. Our prescription? Do something completely out of the ordinary. Travel somewhere new, take a hot air balloon ride, volunteer at a homeless shelter, or get a massage.

- Make it a goal to find a balance between the predictable and the new.

CARPE DIEM:
What can you do today to shake up your routine
or experience something brand new?

52.

DROP THE COMPLAINING

*"If you ask what is the single most important key to longevity,
I would have to say it is avoiding worry, stress, and tension."*
— George Burns

- As Kirby's granddad once said, "Getting old is hell, but the alternative is not very good either." Yes, there are many indignities of aging, but if we focus on the negatives, we miss out on the positives.

- It's easy to fall into a habit of complaining, especially if you have a partner or friend who supports you in it. Yet complaining leaves you feeling empty and irritable. The more you complain, the more things bother you, giving you more to complain about. See where this is going? It's a curmudgeonly cycle. Soon, you'll find yourself barking at store clerks, scolding other drivers, and making a big deal of little errors your family members make.

- The only way to break the cycle is to make a conscious effort to do so. Make a point to listen to yourself and your negative thoughts. Replace judging thoughts with kind ones. Maybe that woman who is tailgating you is late for an important job interview. Maybe the store clerk just found out she's getting laid off and needs your kindness. Make room for the unknown, and assume everyone means well.

- Don't become the cliché of a grouchy, complaining old codger. Smile, look around you, and be thankful for the life you have.

CARPE DIEM:
Today, notice which situations trigger your complaints.
Are they ever more about your own dissatisfaction or
sadness than what's actually happening around you?

53.

(RE)DEFINE YOUR PRIORITIES

*"The key is not to prioritize what's on your
schedule, but to schedule your priorities."*
— Stephen Covey

• A false yet popular belief is that important and successful people
are always busy and make a lot of money. We tend to judge each
other by how much money we earn, what designer clothes we
wear, which car we drive, and what house we own. These are signs
of success.

• Yet the cost of living this belief is that you won't have time or
peace of mind for what's really important: connecting with others
and experiencing self-actualization—fulfilling your truest and
deepest desires, purposes, talents, dreams, and needs. Your life
will lack meaning and feel empty. Think about the super wealthy,
"successful" people you know. Do many of them seem lost?

• Age bring perspective. From your vantage point, it becomes easier
to see that you need to dedicate yourself to becoming a whole
person—one with a balanced body, mind, and soul.

• Tap into this wisdom. Know your priorities. Start by asking
yourself what gives your life meaning, and build your daily
schedule from there. Resist sacrificing your health—physical,
intellectual, emotional, social, and spiritual—for a few more
dollars or a few more turned heads. If your life looks good on the
outside, it doesn't mean it feels good on the inside. Dare to design
your own life.

CARPE DIEM:
If you were told you had just a few weeks to live,
what would you do? That's a clue to your priorities.
Journal or talk this through with someone today.

54.

EMBRACE THE FEAR OF BEING ALONE

*"What a lovely surprise to finally discover
how unlonely being alone can be."*
— Ellen Burstyn

- For some, it is not dying that brings about fear but living alone, then dying alone. Especially for single people, or those who have lost their families, the thought of living alone through the aging process or dying without a loved at their side seems cruel.

- It can be hard for aging single seniors. Who will help them when they become physically or mentally frail? Who will get groceries, mow the lawn, or maintain the house if they can't? These fears and concerns are real and demand solutions.

- As you enter your later years, explore resources in your city for seniors. Many human service and government programs are available for seniors, such as Meals on Wheels and senior centers. Some local hospitals have outreach programs to help seniors manage their healthcare needs.

- Don't be afraid to ask for help. Many neighbors or friends would gladly step in if they knew you were lonely or needed assistance. We know someone whose great uncle lived alone at 90. The woman who groomed his poodle took it upon herself to help him—somehow without challenging his pride. She made him meals and helped clean his home. Trust, and accept, the kindness of strangers, caregivers, friends, and far-away extended family.

CARPE DIEM:
Who do you know right now that would help you? Call that person today and invite her to have lunch or coffee so you can talk.

55.

BE HONEST WITH YOURSELF

"Awareness requires a rapture with the world we take for granted."
— Shoshana Zuboff

- To grow old with grace and confidence, you first must take a good, hard look at yourself. Face yourself with honesty rather than condemnation. Who is your authentic self? What persona do you put on in public or with certain people? Why? Do you have unfinished business to take care of—an apology you'd like to make or a relationship you'd like to mend? Getting honest with yourself—without judgment—will make growing older less frightening.

- Challenge yourself to be authentic in your relations to others. Doing so honors who you are—the good, bad, and not-so-pretty. Owning past hurts you may have caused others or yourself helps wash you clean. Fessing up to a mistake or error (along with a good dose of self-forgiveness) helps you release regrets and pain. When you begin to be honest with yourself, you develop a genuine gut level of truth.

- Beginning to dismantle fear is one of the greatest gifts you can give yourself. To do this you must own your truth. In this way you'll conquer fear rather than suppress it. It sounds odd, but you must learn to befriend your fears and hurts. Doing so will let you age with integrity and grace.

CARPE DIEM:

Make a list of the fears you have about aging. What can you do to avoid running from these fears and be able to smile at them instead?

56.

ENJOY A GOOD LAUGH

"The human race has only one really effective
weapon—and that's laughter."

— Mark Twain

• Humor is one of the most healing gifts of humanity. Numerous studies have shown the physical and emotional benefits of laughter. Humor has been reported to speed healing, strengthen the immune system, and increase our pain thresholds.

• Laughter restores hope and assists in surviving the pain of grief. It helps us feel peace in both mind and body.

• Who in your life makes you laugh? Who can you be most silly or goofy with? Who tells the best jokes or plays the hardest? Spend more time with these people.

• Watch funny movies. Listen to comedians on your iPod. Go to comedy shows.

• Remember the fun times of life. Remember your sense of humor and times you made others split a gut

• Don't get caught up in the seriousness of aging. Laugh at your own foibles. Embrace the wisdom of aging. Know that no one is perfect and we all make mistakes. The lost keys, the frequent trips to the bathroom, the graying hair, and even the incontinence is funny in the right light. Confess your aging secrets to a good friend and share a giggle together in a restaurant booth. You'll be happier for it.

CARPE DIEM:
Close your eyes and remember the smile
and laughter of your best friend.

57.

CHOOSE HAPPINESS

"What I learned from interviewing over 1,500 older Americans is that happiness is a choice, not a condition."
— Karl Pillemer

- Contrary to common beliefs, the Legacy Project found that most elders are happy—a fact proven through thousands of interviews.

- Happiness, health, and compassionate living seemed to be the themes that allowed older adults to continue to live life fully, no matter what their age.

- How about you? Are you grateful for your life? Do you feel satisfied with yourself and others?

- Think small when it comes to happiness. We tend to think of happiness as an emotional high, a special-occasion emotion reserved for when we realize lofty goals or obtain a cherished possession. Yet it's the little things in our days that bring us happiness—watching the birds at the feeder, sharing a smile with a neighbor, enjoying a good meal.

- To quote a 79-year-old we know: "Take each day and live it and love it. It might be your very last day here. Don't be aggravated, don't aggravate anybody else, and just keep a smile on your face. You'll be happier and everyone around you will be, too." And remember the words of Ruth Ann Schabacker, who once said, "Each day comes bearing gifts. Untie the ribbons."

CARPE DIEM:
Each night, say a gratitude prayer. List all the good things that happened during the day, and name what you are grateful for.

58.

FOLLOW YOUR STAR

"Aim for the moon. If you miss, you may hit a star."
— W. Clement Stone

- One huge perk of growing older is that you have gained wisdom through years of living. Wisdom is the language of your authentic self.

- With wisdom comes perspective. Now that we are older we often find ourselves on familiar ground—we understand how to face sadness, gather strength and courage in the face of a challenge, and support others in their journeys. Not too much rattles us anymore.

- If you are going down a path that feels unsatisfying, use your wisdom to figure out what's missing. Are you living a mundane life that's too familiar and isn't challenging you to grow or use your strengths? Are you lonely and need companionship? Listen to your heart. Let it guide you on where to go, what to do. Listen above the crowd.

- Like the Magi, or wise men, who followed the star and found the baby Jesus, follow your star. Combat self-judgment that says, "I am too old" or, "I will get too tired." Following your own star is about discovering who you are and what you are capable of. It's embracing yourself fully. Your chance at greatness is intrinsically linked to being yourself. It's never too late. Follow your star and you'll find yourself.

CARPE DIEM:
Listen to the wisdom of your heart. What would
you like to bring into your life, right now?

59.

TRUST YOUR JOURNEY

"Dream as if you'll live forever. Live as if you'll die today."
— James Dean

- Your life has had its ups and downs, but it has brought you to where you are today. Don't question your journey. Trust that you took the right path—the one you needed to take to learn all the lessons in life that you needed to learn.

- No doubt, you can look back and see places where you could have gone another way. What if you had married a different person? Chosen a different career? Lived in a different town? If you believe that we seek out the experiences we need to grow into who we are, then all those possible outcomes don't matter. You are on your right journey.

- We all have weakness or traits we'd like to change. At some time we wished we were smarter or more successful or acted differently. It's important to stay focused on the positive outcomes of your life so far. Relish in your merits and resist being pulled down by your perceived faults. If you feel that downward current tugging, change your situation fast. Call a friend, get out in the sunshine, or count your blessings. It's been a rich journey, and you get to create the final leg.

CARPE DIEM:
Relax into yourself today.

60.

NEVER STOP DANCING

- After a bomb killed two dozen young people at a Tel Aviv disco a few years ago, Israeli youth refused to be cowed. They resumed a robust nightlife. Beneath a stone memorial listing the names of the dead is a single inscription: LO NAFSEEK LIRKOD. It means, "We won't stop dancing."

- Life challenges can beat us down. Losses and hardships make us stop dancing or, worse yet, forget that dancing is even possible.

- Don't lose your desire to dance. The music is still playing. The tune may be different, but there is still reason to dance. To put it in Shakespearean terms, despite the slings and arrow of outrageous fortune, we should never stop dancing.

- Your body has changed and will continue to change. Make adjustments and keep moving. There are wonders out there waiting to be explored. Your life is a vast landscape painting— much of it is filled in with fine details, but there is still some blank canvas. Decide which details and colors you want to add and do it. Tap into the colors of joy, peace, happiness, and satisfaction

- Don't be cowed by the "bombs and the terror" of aging. Life has purpose at every age.

- Enjoy life. Find meaning. Dance.

CARPE DIEM:
Do something "dancy" today, just because.

STAYING SOCIALLY
CONNECTED AS YOU AGE

"Old friends pass away, new friends appear. It is just like the days.
An old day passes, a new day arrives. The important thing is to
make it meaningful: a meaningful friend or a meaningful day."

— Dalai Lama

If you're socially active, you've probably got the other bases covered. After all, if you're regularly doing things like volunteering, going out to lunch with friends, and playing cards with your grandkids, you're also staying physically, intellectually, and emotionally active, right?

Yes, many people believe (and research supports this) that staying connected to neighbors, friends, and family is the key not only to longevity but to good quality of life in our later years. Our relationships bring us joy and make life worth living.

So if you're not a "joiner" or a "social butterfly," we urge you to step outside your comfort zone and work at getting involved socially. Participate in clubs or organizations, and reach out to friends and family. Your body, brain, heart, and spirit will thank you for it.

61.

KEEP FAMILY CLOSE

"Family is not an important thing. It's everything."
— Michael J. Fox

- Relationships that stand the test of time are often with family. They were at our sides when we were nine, and they'll be there when we're 90. The faces might change, but family is a constant force throughout our lives for most of us. Keep your family close.

- Granted, relationships within families are not always easy. It can seem like no matter how old you grow, you're stuck in the role you played in your family of origin—the baby, the boss, or the bully. It's how your siblings and parents see you.

- If you find this is true for you, it's time to redefine your relationships with family. If you haven't seen your brother in a long time, arrange a visit. Seeing each other one-on-one, without other family members present, will give you a chance to get to know the grown-up versions of each other.

- Also, work to form relationships with the younger generation— your nieces, nephews, and grandchildren. It's important for them to get a different perspective on life than what their immediate family can offer, and they can give you the extended care and concern of family in your later years.

CARPE DIEM:
Is there a family member you haven't seen or talked
to in a while? Connect with him or her today.

62.

CHERISH YOUR FRIENDS

*"Since there is nothing so well worth having as
friends, never lose a chance to make them."*
— Francesco Guicciardini

- Friends are your other family—your family of choice. Often, our friends know us better than our siblings do.

- Cherish your friends, especially those who have journeyed with you through the years, sticking by you during both hard and easy times. Make it a habit to connect with these friends regularly.

- True friendships strike a perfect balance of give and take. Sometimes she lifts you up, other times you lift her up. Your friendship isn't limited to one activity or a few topics—you can do anything together, and share both laughter and tears. In the end, if you have even one friend who feels like a sister or brother, you're lucky.

- Share with your friends your feelings of grief about aging. Commiserate together, laugh together.

- Being a good friend starts with you. People are comfortable around friends who are honest, sincere, and open. Respect your friend's boundaries and try to stay positive. Be a good listener.

- Finding friends is easier than you might expect. Talk to someone at church, ask a coworker to lunch, join a team sport, or chat with neighbors.

CARPE DIEM:
Invite a friend, acquaintance, or colleague to lunch this week.

63.

REACH OUT AND TOUCH SOMEONE

*"Every day you should reach out and touch someone. People
love a warm hug, or just a friendly pat on the back."*
— Maya Angelou

• For many people, physical contact with another human being is
healing. Touching has been recognized since ancient times to have
transformative, healing powers. Touch often replaces words when
words are inadequate. Touch is the universal language of love and
support.

• Have you hugged anyone lately? Held someone's hand? Put your
arm around a friend? Walked arm and arm with a neighbor? Held
a child on your lap? Snuggled a baby?

• You probably know several people who enjoy hugging or physical
touching. If you're comfortable with their touch, encourage it in
the weeks and months to come. Touching soothes the soul and
makes you feel connected.

• Getting a massage is another way to receive healing touch.
Schedule an appointment for a full body massage today, or, if this
makes you uncomfortable, just your neck and shoulders.

CARPE DIEM:
Hug a close friend or family member today, even if you usually don't.

64.

MOURN YOUR LOVED ONES' DEATHS

"Once a week there's some sort of bad news. Once a month
there's a funeral. You lose close friends and discover one
of the worst truths of old age: they're irreplaceable."
— Nora Ephron

• As you grow older, you may find that you attend funeral after funeral. This might make you feel vulnerable, as if death is working its way through your circle of friends and will be knocking on your door soon, too.

• Accept this feeling as real then soothe it by redirecting your energies toward mourning the deaths of those you care about. One way to actively mourn is to honor their lives by emulating their best traits. Was your classmate quick with a joke? Did your Aunt Mary always have a kind word to share? Adopt their ways of being.

• Maybe you have lost a spouse, parent, or child and your grief runs especially deep. Embrace the pain of your loss. It is easier to turn away or avoid your hard feelings, but journeying through them will help you integrate the death and find healing. During this time, you need support. Reach out to a friend, family member, or support group and share your grief.

• You can only mourn so much, especially in the early days after a death. Allow yourself breaks—take "doses" of grief, then rest. Honor where you are in the process and be gentle with yourself.

CARPE DIEM:
Get in touch with your true feelings of grief over a recent death.

65.

GRIEVE YOUR PERSONAL LOSSES

"The other day, on the computer, I pulled up something I
wrote three years ago, and it was written in a type so small
I can't imagine how I wrote the thing in the first place."
— Nora Ephron

• Just as when you lose someone you love, you also feel personal losses as you age. These are often small (such as minor memory lapses) but sometimes they are large, repeated, and progressive losses that occur during your later years.

• You may find that you are unable to do things you once could easily do. You may also lose friends and family to death, or maybe you are losing your health and possibly your sense of security. These losses add up, and you can find yourself feeling lost or depressed.

• Have you experienced any of these losses that come with aging? It's important to name them and mourn them, no matter how silly or inconsequential they might seem. If you have experienced a large loss—like your physical health or the death of someone loved—seek out support from others, both friends and professionals.

• As best you can, replace lost activities with similar ones. For example, if you can't play basketball anymore, attend local games at the high school and cheer on the team. Or maybe you can help coach!

• Honor your ever-changing journey. Your life may not be as it was before, but new joys await you.

CARPE DIEM:
Sit down with pen and paper and make a list of your
personal losses with aging. In the coming days, take all
the time you need to mourn each one's passing.

66.

HEAL PAST WOUNDS

"In every community, there is work to be done. In every nation, there are wounds to heal. In every heart, there is the power to do it."
— Marianne Williamson

- Is there someone in your life with whom you used to be close but now are not? Is there pain around the relationship, or have you released it completely?

- Did you have a falling out with a sibling, or did you drift away from a best friend?

- If you carry hurt about a past conflict or split with another person and you miss the relationship on some level, work to heal that past wound.

- Most likely, if you approach the person with compassion and a true openness to forgiveness or making amends, you will be well received. Speak from the "I" point of view. Tell her how you feel about the loss and what you miss about the relationship. The conflict doesn't have to be resolved. You can agree to disagree and emphasize rebuilding the connection around what works between the two of you.

- Having friends and a rewarding social network has been shown to extend lifespan and improve health. Create and keep meaningful relationships in your life.

CARPE DIEM:
Who used to be in your life whom you valued but no longer have contact with? Can you reconnect with that person?

67.

TAP INTO YOUR HEART

*"The heart is like a garden. It can grow compassion or fear,
resentment or love. What seeds will you plant there?"*
— the Buddha

• Pema Chodron, a Buddhist nun, uses the story about building a
Buddhist monastery to illustrate tapping into human goodness.
While digging the foundation for the retreat center, the builders
hit bedrock. Work came to a standstill, but soon a small crack
appeared. A minute later there was water dripping out, and an
hour later the crack was wider and the flow was stronger, until
soon water was gushing from the rocks. The water was a welcome
surprise and became a center point of healing for the monastery.

• Tapping into your heart is like tapping into a spring of living water
that has been temporarily encased in rock.

• When you acknowledge your aging process and mourn your losses,
you touch the center of your sorrow. You sit with discomfort
without trying to fix it. You stay open to the pain and let it soften
you. These are the times you connect with your own open-hearted
goodness. It is by feeling your pain that you open your heart to
the world.

• Tapping into this shaky and tender place has a transformative
effect. It opens your heart to yourself and to others. While you
may feel vulnerable, this is when you are most open to receive, and
give, love.

CARPE DIEM:
Make space to invite the tender, vulnerable side of yourself to come
forward. Sit in nature, listen to meaningful music, or meditate.

68.

MAKE A DIFFERENCE

*"The human contribution is the essential ingredient. It is
only in the giving of oneself to others that we truly live."*
— Ethel Percy Andrus

• A great way to get out of ourselves and into the world is to
volunteer. Helping others or advancing a good cause adds
meaning to our lives.

• Studies have shown that people who volunteer are more happy and
satisfied with their lives. It taps into their humanity by allowing
them to act with empathy and compassion toward others.

• Volunteering is also a great way to be social and meet people with
similar interests. Digging in and working together side-by-side
creates a unique sense of unity and purpose.

• Is there a local human service agency that you admire? Maybe a
women's shelter or a food bank? Do you have skills to offer, say
carpentry to Habitat for Humanity or trail building to the park
service?

• What are your social values? How can you support one of these
through volunteering?

CARPE DIEM:
Visit your local United Way office or peruse the want ads for
volunteer opportunities in your local newspaper. Consider human
service agencies, hospital, schools, and places of worship.

69.

MAKE CHANGE HAPPEN

"The world won't change until I change."
— James Cowan

- Just as volunteering is satisfying, so is working to better your community.

- Often, change is motivated by one person's dissatisfaction or desire to make something better. One little action can get the ball rolling, and before you know it you've created significant social change.

- What is bugging you these days? Maybe it's the traffic congestion. In Fort Collins, Colorado, where we live, an engineer at the local university couldn't stand how he'd always seem to hit a red light on the main road through town, so he designed a system to better coordinate stoplights and shared it with City engineers.

- Maybe you can't do something on such a large scale, but you can call the City or County, voice your opinion about something that's wrong, and suggest ways to make it right. Or you can join a committee or board designed to solve a problem at your work, place of worship, social group, or neighborhood.

- Participating in making change happen and improving a situation is empowering. It taps into the knowledge, wisdom, and ability of your life experiences; it makes age an asset that you can wield for the common good.

CARPE DIEM:
In what ways, big and small, could your community improve? How can you help make that happen?

70.

COMFORT A FRIEND

"Don't walk behind me; I may not lead. Don't walk in front of me; I may not follow. Just walk beside me and be my friend."
— Albert Camus

- Life is full of ups and downs. Sometimes we, and those we care for, coast along. That is, until we hit a rut or lose a wheel.

- If a friend of yours is going through a rough patch, be there for him or her.

- If he is experiencing an illness, comfort him by offering rides to the doctor, making meals, doing his laundry, or offering kind words and an open ear.

- If she has lost a loved one to death, go beyond sending a card or bringing food. Make a conscious effort to get in touch regularly during the coming weeks and months. Offer words of comfort during holidays and anniversaries. Don't fall into the trap of thinking you don't want to bring up the person who died for fear of causing sad feelings. Most likely, that person is on your friend's mind most of the time anyway. Hearing someone acknowledge her loss makes her feel less alone.

- When it comes to giving support, friends and family tend to break down into a "law of thirds." One third of the people offer support, another third remain neutral, and a final third are negative or hurtful. Be in the first third whenever you can.

CARPE DIEM:
Do you know someone who is having a hard time? Reach out and show your support.

71.

JOIN A SENIOR CENTER

*"Beautiful young people are accidents of nature,
but beautiful old people are works of art."*
— Eleanor Roosevelt

- Across the U.S. are 15,000 senior centers. Most likely, there's one in your town. Have you visited it yet?

- Senior centers provide programs and activities for seniors— people generally 55 years of age and older. Some senior centers promote independent living by offering referrals to agencies that can provide financial support, housing assistance, meals, rides, and more to keep seniors in their own homes.

- Don't think of your local senior center as a place for old people. More and more, senior centers cater to all adults and sometimes even to families. You'll likely find young people mixed in with older people in the pool, gym, or meeting rooms.

- Of course, senior centers are great places to meet interesting people and make new friends. Many also offer several social groups to join.

- The National Council on Aging touts research showing that older adults who are involved in senior center programs experience marked improvements in their social, physical, emotional, spiritual, mental, and economic well-being. Consider joining yours today.

CARPE DIEM:
If you haven't already, explore your local senior center.

72.

USE SOCIAL MEDIA TO STAY IN TOUCH

"Social media is about sociology and psychology more than technology."

— Brian Solis

- Facebook is a popular social tool with older Americans today. It lets people share photos of themselves and their families as well as thoughts on everyday happenings or political and social events. While this may seem like mere boasting or self-centered drivel at first, it has a deeper, more important purpose—it keeps people connected to friends and family and helps people feel less lonely.

- The same is true for using smart phones for texting or computers for instant messaging. These simple tools allow you to immediately connect with someone and share a brief message. Some people argue against such communications, wanting people to just "pick up the phone"! Yet each of these forms of communication has its own value and purpose. Texting lets you connect without interrupting. Emailing lets you share thoughts, photos, and documents on a personal level. Facebook keeps you "in the loop," and LinkedIn allows professionals to network with people in their field.

- One caveat: Learn the social norms around what information is appropriate for each outlet. Letting others know someone is gravely ill, for example, is almost always most appropriate face-to-face or over the phone.

CARPE DIEM:

If you don't use social media to connect with others, consider doing so. It's a great way to reconnect with old friends and colleagues and stay current with far-flung family.

73.

CONNECT WITH OLD CLASSMATES

*"Middle age is when your old classmates are so gray
and wrinkled and bald they don't recognize you."*

— Bennett Cerf (get it?)

• It never ceases to amaze us when we hear stories of how a
divorced person, or someone whose spouse has died, connected
with an old classmate and now hang out and enjoy each other or
get married. It seems like a common occurrence.

• Old classmates hold a special place in our lives. Maybe it's because
we shared our formative years together. There is a sense of home
with old classmates and friends.

• As you age, you might think fondly back on your school days.
If so, make it a point to reconnect with those old friends who
mattered most. Google their names and you might be looking
at their Facebook within minutes. Contact them and get
reacquainted.

• Attend class reunions, or plan a trip during homecoming to your
alma mater. Go with your old college buddies and explore some
of your favorite haunts. A lot of memories will come flowing
back and you'll have a blast reminiscing about them all.

CARPE DIEM:
What is your best friend from high school doing these days? Make
it a point to connect with him or her soon, preferably in person.

74.

JOIN A SOCIAL CLUB

*"A friend is one of the nicest things you can have,
and one of the best things you can be."*
— Douglas Pagels

• One advantage of growing older is having more free time. In our 50s, our kids often leave home and life settles down. In our 60s we might retire, freeing up even more time. In our 70s and 80s we might wind down a bit and prefer to spend more time closer to home.

• So what do you do with all the extra time on your hands?

• Joining a social club not only fills your time with a meaningful venture, it also wards off the loneliness you might feel from losing people to moving, death, or different life directions.

• There are social groups for almost everything. There are clubs for hiking, biking, knitting, running, gardening, golfing, traveling, reading, writing, exercising, photography, helping the community (Lion's Club, Sertoma), and more. There are study groups, bible groups, book groups, current event groups, retired professional groups, and so on.

• Senior centers, churches, and city and county offices are great places to explore which clubs are available in your community.

CARPE DIEM:
What are your hobbies or interests? Find a club that focuses on one of these activities and attend an upcoming meeting. If it helps, ask a friend or acquaintance if they are in a club and tag along.

75.

HAVE LUNCH ON FRIDAYS

"Ask not what you can do for your country. Ask what's for lunch."
— Orson Welles

- It's fun and important to have standing dates with friends. Regular get-togethers give structure to your week. For example, maybe you and your neighbor friends could have lunch on Fridays.

- It doesn't have to be lunch. How about a commitment to play golf on Saturdays with a group of people, and whoever shows up, shows up?

- Or maybe you and your spouse and another couple have a plan to try a different restaurant on the last Friday of each month, or you and a group of friends get together to play cards every Sunday.

- What's important is not so much the activity but the consistent commitment to spend time with friends or family.

- As you grow older, having built-in commitments with others is important. They act as a buoy during times of change, offering a constant for you to rely upon. They also create an easy outlet for enjoyment.

CARPE DIEM:
What activity sounds fun to do with friends? It can be goofy—like karaoke—or purposeful, like volunteering. Brainstorm which fun activity you'd like to bring into your life on a regular basis and suggest it to a few friends.

76.

GET A PET

"All of the animals except man know that the principal business of life is to enjoy it."
— Samuel Butler

- According to a recent study by the American Psychological Association, pet owners had "greater self-esteem, were more physically fit, less lonely, more conscientious, more extroverted, less fearful, and tended to be less preoccupied" compared to non-pet owners.

- Studies also show that petting an animal lowers blood pressure and stress.

- Do you have a dog or cat? Animals are great companions. Dogs give unconditional love and opportunities to get out and walk. Cats offer silky soft fur to stroke and a comforting purring sound to relax to.

- When a spouse dies, some elderly people find great comfort in their pets. Pets can be a link to their spouse as well as providing a sense of family and companionship.

- Many older people don't want to be tied down by a pet or worry about having a pet outlive them. Both these worries have solutions. Neighbor kids often love earning money caring for your animal while you travel (and kennels are another good solution). If you're concerned about a pet's lifespan, consider selecting an older animal at the shelter who will have less energy and fewer years ahead.

CARPE DIEM:

If you don't want to take on a pet, is there a neighbor dog you can offer to walk or care for in a family's absence? Does a friend have a pet you can enjoy?

77.

BEFRIEND YOUR NEIGHBORS

"By ourselves we can enjoy life, but to really
appreciate life we must find companionship."

— Anonymous

- As you age, it's especially important to connect with your neighbors, who can be a great resource and comfort.

- Being friendly with your neighbors provides a sense of security. When someone knows you, they tend to watch out for you and your house. If you leave on vacation, you can rest assured someone's keeping an eye on your house and property.

- There's a nice give-and-take with neighbors. They pull your trash down to the curb when you go away, and you do the same for them. You can exchange animal care or plant watering needs.

- As you get into your later years, neighbors can help you stay independent in your home longer. Some don't mind picking up a few groceries for you when they do their own shopping or bringing you along when they go. Don't be afraid to ask for help.

- Make it a point to stop and talk with your neighbors when you see them out. Socialize on walks, invite them over for coffee, and hire their kids for small jobs, like dog walking or raking leaves.

- Accept the help of neighbors, and relish in the sense of community that knowing your neighbors brings.

CARPE DIEM:
Are you friendly with your neighbors on either side of you? If not, make an effort to get to know them better.

78.

SHARE YOUR STORIES

*"Storytelling is the most powerful way to
put ideas into the world today."*
— Robert McKee

- A value of old age is that you have a lot of experience and stories to share. Telling your stories benefits both you and others.

- You may find that memories come rushing back to you at certain times. Try to capture these memories by writing them down or telling them to someone else—a friend, neighbor, niece, nephew, coworker, or co-volunteer.

- Most people find life stories to be fascinating. What got you from there to here? How did you meet and marry your spouse? What was it like growing up where you did, and in your particular family? How did you advance in your career? As long as you keep your stories contained and relatively short, others will enjoy listening to you.

- Maybe you want to capture your life story, but it feels like too much to write it or type it yourself. Can you dictate it to your daughter-in-law or a friend? She can ask you questions about your life, and you can tell her what happened in a chronological order, hitting the highlights. When you are done, you will have a recorded piece of personal history.

CARPE DIEM:
Make it a point to share a personal story with someone today.
Telling others your stories helps you make sense of your life.

79.

TEACH A SKILL

"Do all the good you can, in all the ways you can, to all the souls you can, in every place you can, at all the times you can, with all the zeal you can, as long as you can."

— John Wesley

- You've learned a lot in your life. Share it.

- What are some skills you have mastered over your lifetime, thus far? Which would you feel comfortable teaching to others?

- You are a wealth of knowledge on certain subjects and skills. Look back on your career and the various jobs you have held. Which skills can you pass on to others?

- Consider sharing your knowledge with school-aged children. For example, you could volunteer as a tutor in the schools or for a nonprofit agency (like the Boys and Girls Club) to help a struggling child learn to read, write, do geometry, or play an instrument. Or, you could introduce a class to a foreign language, an art form, or car mechanics.

- You could also help a particular young person succeed in life. Consider becoming a Big Brother/Big Sister volunteer, or teaching a skills at a local program for teens in trouble.

- Sharing your knowledge with others helps you to age confidently and with purpose.

CARPE DIEM:
Call your local school district and ask about volunteer opportunities.

80.

WEAR MICKEY MOUSE EARS, IF THAT'S WHAT YOU WANT TO DO

"We don't stop playing because we grow old;
we grow old because we stop playing."
— George Bernard Shaw

- On a recent airline flight we noticed a couple in their thirties with matching Mickey and Minnie Mouse ears getting on the plane. At first we were taken aback. What foolishness! Why would adults be acting like children? But then it dawned on us: if you are going to Disneyland, why not wear Mickey Mouse ears?

- Life is enjoyable no matter what age we happen to be. Stepping outside the societal rules for our age means allowing ourselves to truly relish in our lives and be authentically ourselves.

- It means letting go of some of the rules we have developed for ourselves and the stereotypes we've adopted about older people and aging.

- One of the benefits of growing older is that you don't care so much anymore about what others think or who might be judging you. You are comfortable in your own skin. If you want to act silly and feel like a kid again, you do it.

- What's the equivalent to Mickey Mouse ears for you?

CARPE DIEM:
Which stereotypes do you have about older people
that hold you back? Which self-definitions are keeping
you stuck? Bust out and enjoy yourself today.

Focusing on Your Spiritual Self As You Age

"In a spiritually sensitive culture, then, it might well be that age is something to be admired or envied."

— Rowan D. Williams

Your spiritual self is who you are deep inside—your innermost essence, stripped of all the external trappings of your life. It is who you were before you took on your earthly form, and it is who you will continue to be after you leave it.

It is your soul, or "divine spark"—what Meister Eckhart described as "that which gives depth and purpose to our living."

It is you without age, for while your physical self does indeed continually change over time, your spiritual self is timeless.

Getting in touch with and nurturing your spiritual self is your life's work. And one of the blessings of age is that when we are older, we finally have the time and the patience to slow down and really listen to that still, small voice inside us.

81.

CREATE A LIFE VISION

"Life is a great big canvas, and you should throw all the paint on it you can."
— Danny Kaye

- The idea of the Golden Years is sweet but often not real. As we age, we are faced with loss and change. Careers end, kids move away, health issues arise, and people we love die.

- If life has thrown you challenges, remember the longevity of life. Try not to get stuck in the unpleasantness of the here and now. Most likely, you've gained the perspective over the years of, "This too shall pass." Practice this spiritual endurance.

- Growing older means you must adjust your life vision. What you knew as constants—work, family unit, health—shifts. Honor these changes by intentionally shifting with them. Create a vision for your life.

- Ask yourself key questions, like: What do I still want to see, do, experience? What type of job, side work, or hobbies do I want? Where do I want to live? Do I want to stay near my family?

- A good starting place is to fill in the phrase, "I want...." Sometimes exploring the opposite—what you don't want—brings clarity. Don't forget to include spiritual wants, such as peace, calm, serenity, and simplicity.

- Now, close your eyes and see yourself in the future fulfilling your wants and your soul's desires.

CARPE DIEM:
Take time to explore your life vision on paper. Be patient. Ideas may come over time.

82.

ADOPT THE EIGHT UNIVERSAL HEALING PRINCIPLES

*"It is only when you have both divine grace and
human endeavor that you can experience bliss."*
— Sri Sathya Sai Baba

• Commit to wellness by adopting eight healing principles, used
in the majority of cultures. These regular habits sustain your
physical, intellectual, emotional, social, and spiritual well-being.

- Eat a balanced diet.
- Get daily exercise.
- Enjoy fun, play, and laughter.
- Experience music, dance, and chanting.
- Have interests, hobbies, and creative outlets.
- Experience love, touch, and support systems.
- Surround yourself with nature, beauty, and a serene
  environment.
- Have faith and belief in the supernatural.

• Let these eight principles guide you as you move through the later
years of your life. If you adopt all of them, you'll experience a
balanced and healthy life.

CARPE DIEM:
Which of these healing principles do you practice daily? Which
are missing? Commit to bringing yourself into balance.

83.

BE PATIENT

"Lord, teach me to be patient with life, with people, with myself. I try to speed things along too much, and I push for results before the time is right. Teach me to trust your sense of timing. Teach me to slow down enough to appreciate life"

— Unknown

- Patience is a sign of being spiritually at peace.

- Patience is an art form. Staying calm when things go wrong or take too long is a refined skill, one that takes practice and a commitment to inner calm. Don't give your calm away to a long line at the post office or road construction.

- As the Tao Te Ching asks, "Can you remain unmoving until the right action arises by itself?"

- Having patience means consciously deciding to address a situation with peace and kindness. Most likely, growing older has strengthened your patience. You've learned to act versus react. You've learned to pause and ponder before talking. You've adopted a wait-and-see approach to tricky situations.

- Remember also to be patient with yourself. If you forget someone's name, be easy on yourself. If you get tired faster than before, go gentle.

CARPE DIEM:
Today, practice patience while talking with loved ones, driving around town, waiting in line, and noticing yourself.

84.

EXPERIENCE THE ELEMENTS

"The air we breathe, the water we drink, and the land we inhabit are not only critical elements in the quality of life we enjoy - they are a reflection of the majesty of our Creator."

— Rick Perry

- Ancient scientists proclaimed the world was made up of four elements: air, earth, fire, and water. By definition, elements are pure, basic, and simple life forces. The four elements can bring comfort and meaning, and help us feel centered in ourselves. They provide sustenance to our bodies and souls. Honor each in the following ways:
  - Air: Breathe deeply. Stand in the wind. Sail. Watch the trees dance.
  - Fire: Light a candle in memory of someone loved. Build a fire in a fireplace or fire pit. Contemplate the dancing flames. Feel the warmth on your skin.
  - Earth: Plant bulbs. Start a compost pile. Dig for worms. Lie in the grass and gaze at the stars.
  - Water: Stand by the ocean. Paddle in a lake. Jump a stream. Take a long bath. Go for a swim. Walk in the rain.
- When experiencing the four elements, slow time down and experience the moment. Feel the power each offers.

CARPE DIEM:

Each of the 12 signs of the zodiac is associated with one of the four elements. Look up your zodiac sign, see which element it represents, and contemplate whether its meaning is true for you.

85.

GO TO THE WATER

*"For whatever we lose (like a you or a me), it's
always ourselves we find in the sea."*

— e.e. cummings

• While all the elements are healing, water is especially so.

• Maybe it's because we floated in water in the womb, or maybe it's
because we are made up of two-thirds water. For whatever reason,
we are often calmed by water—the serenity of a quiet pond, the
trickling of a mountain stream, the rush of a waterfall.

• Seek out opportunities to be near water. Sit still and take in
how the light dances on the water's surface. Experience this
affirmation: "Water is pure; water is healing; water is life." Let
water remind you of the deep pool that resides inside you.

• Have you walked in the rain lately? Remember being a kid and
feeling warm rain pelt your face and body? Remember the thrill
that ran through you? Rain on the roof makes a wonderful sound.
The pitter-patter of rain is comforting and can lull us into a sense
of peace. Rain is refreshing. Symbolically, it washes us clean. It
renews us and fills us with hope.

• Feel the renewal of water.

CARPE DIEM:
Visit a body of water sometime within the next few days. Sit in
peace and enjoy the sights and sounds of your surroundings.

86.

GET OUT

"Man's heart away from nature becomes hard."
— Standing Bear

• Spending time in nature is soothing and restoring. Have you ever noticed how looking at beautiful scenery, hearing the sounds of birds, and feeling the sun on your face makes you let out a sigh, release your troubles, and turn toward the positive?

• As a human being you are part of the natural world. A close relationship with nature grounds your psyche and soul in the spiritual certainty of your roots. If you lose touch with nature's rhythms, you lose touch with your deepest self—what has been called "the ground of being."

• Get out in nature every day. You don't have to travel to a national park and sit in awe of nature's treasures to gain benefits—yet it certainly is fun to do sometimes. Often, being in your own backyard or at a neighborhood park can restore you

• Watch clouds form. Gaze at stars. Stand barefoot in the cool grass. Play in the snow. Taste sweet strawberries in the field. Feel Mother Nature soothe your soul, calm your body, and refresh your spirit.

• In the Celtic tradition, "thin places" are places where the separation between the physical world and the spiritual world become tenuous—where water and land meet or land and sky come together. Seek out these places and contemplate the holy.

CARPE DIEM:
Go for a walk in nature today and invite peace,
tranquility, and the Divine to come along.

87.

LIVE SIMPLY

"You can't have everything. Where would you put it?"
— Steven Wright

- There's an underground movement in America to live simply. It's in response to the gluttony we can show—having multiple houses and cars, owning loads of stuff, and using a lot of resources.

- Living simply not only helps the earth, it helps us. The less clutter and complication we have in managing our things, the less clutter and complication we feel in our minds and souls.

- Living simply fits well with growing older. As you age, you probably yearn for simplicity. You slow down, both physically and mentally. You may not be able to function well enough to keep up with a busy, demanding schedule. Trying to can lead to stress and frustration.

- Accept where you are. If you are physically ailing, adjust your lifestyle. Slow down. If being with too many people makes you worry about forgetting names or being socially correct, surround yourself with loving friends and family instead.

- Consider the following to simplify your life: Take your name off junk mail lists, forego optional meetings and obligatory social events, and give away items you no longer like or need. If you can afford to, hire others to tend to your lawn and gardens or clean your house.

CARPE DIEM:
How can you live more simply, starting today?

88.

BE KIND

"My religion is kindness."
— Dalai Lama

- Buddhists believe in "loving kindness practice," which has been passed down in an unbroken line for over 2,500 years and helps people develop a mental habit of selflessness and altruistic love. It is similar to other religious teachings that promote loving others as ourselves.

- Before we can love others, we must love ourselves—a common yet true saying.

- Show love to yourself by making your happiness a priority. You've come to an age where you can drop the endless self-pressure to perform, get everything done, and take care of everyone else's needs before your own. Taking time for your own needs is certainly an important first step in creating "loving kindness."

- Yet your happiness can't come at the expense of others. This will ring hollow. True happiness comes from feeling unity with others, seeing them as fellow humans on a similar journey. Thank your grocery bagger, say hi when passing a stranger on the street, hold the door, and smile. When you are kind, you receive kindness in return, usually more than expected.

CARPE DIEM:
Have you shown yourself loving kindness recently? In what ways could you take care better care of yourself today?

89.

MEDITATE, VISUALIZE

"Breathe. Let go. And remind yourself that this very moment is the only one you know you have for sure."

— Oprah Winfrey

• Yes, the changes that come with aging can be stressful. Counter your stress with meditation and visualization.

• The aim of meditation is to bring inner peace. It's like shutting the door on the world and retreating, for a while, into the cool silence of your Self.

• Sit in a quiet, comfortable place with legs crossed or in the lotus position. If desired, play calming music. Take several deep, steady breaths and clear your mind. If thoughts enter your mind, release them and concentrate on your breathing or on a positive word or short phrase. Be patient, as the mind does not always want to focus. With regular practice you can gain a wonderful sense of yourself and feel at peace. Meditation is a way to self-heal and replace tension and dis-ease with peace and calm.

• Visualization is like taking a mental vacation. It frees your mind while keeping your body in a calm state. Often when you are anxious, your thoughts turn negative. By creating a positive picture of yourself in soothing surroundings—where you watch everything you do turn out right and bring joy—you can restore yourself to a positive state.

CARPE DIEM:
Try meditating or visualizing a few minutes each day at a certain time, say upon waking or going to bed. After a week, consider if it helps calm you. If so, keep at it!

90.

RISE ABOVE

"A man is not old until regrets take the place of dreams."
— John Barrymore

- It's hard to realize that more life is behind you than in front of you. You may fall into the trap of thinking you haven't done enough with your life, or that you are now too old to fall in love, to dance, to wear a swimsuit, and so on. Make an effort to rise above your own self-judgments and society's misconceptions about what older people can and can't do.

- Release any inner pressure that says you must "leave your mark" when you die. At funerals, guests rarely talk about the person's accomplishments with work and wealth. What they do talk about is character—how kind, generous, and loving a person was. Trust that you already have left your mark with those you love—and if you haven't, it's not too late to start being kind, generous, and loving. If you want to do good in the world, by all means do so. During these last years, focus on creating meaning and happiness in your life for yourself and others, and you will certainly leave your mark.

- Also, challenge society's idea that being young is more important than being old. Show the world that you have value—maybe even more so—in your later years. Share your wisdom, knowledge, love, and patience.

- Take on this motto: Forget about dying with dignity. Live with dignity!

CARPE DIEM:
Tap into the idea that today is a gift, and live it like it's
your last—doing what matters and what brings joy.

91.

BE STILL

*"Happiness is not a matter of intensity but of
balance, order, rhythm, and harmony."*
— Thomas Merton

• It's easy to be busy. Being busy makes us feel like life has purpose.
Also, if we stay busy, we feel young.

• It's not wrong to be busy, but as with everything, it's best to strike
a balance. If most of your days don't allow you time to simply sit
still and relax or contemplate, then it's time to cut a few things out
of your schedule.

• When you are constantly busy, you can't hear messages from your
emotional self or your soul. If you feel grief over losses brought
on by aging, your busyness may seem like an excuse to avoid these
feelings. Yet ignoring your feelings will prolong your grief, and
turning away from your soul will make you feel lost and off center.

• Do you often feel irritable or impatient? That's a sign that you are
doing too much and not taking time to open to your inner realm.

• Take time to sit quietly by yourself every day—check in with
your feelings, and consider their origin. Ask yourself, "What do I
need, right now?" It's vital that during this time you unplug from
television, the internet, your phone, computer games, and all other
modern distractions.

CARPE DIEM:
Taking time for a glass of iced tea on the back porch was
something our rural ancestors understood as valuable.
Can you do something similar on a regular basis?

92.

FIND MAGIC IN THE EVERYDAY

*"Happiness is the meaning and purpose of life, the
whole aim and end of human existence."*
— Aristotle

• Finding magic in the everyday is about relishing all the good things
in your life—your loving relationships, your home and garden,
your pets, your hobbies, your contributions to society and others,
and your own health and wellbeing.

• Finding magic is keeping up with everything that works well in
your life. It's eating well, exercising, having a positive attitude,
making good choices, and staying in touch with your needs and
feelings. All these things bring balance, happiness, and peace—and
that's downright magical.

• Live life with a sense of urgency. Yes, we all procrastinate. And
procrastination isn't usually a big deal when it comes to the little
things. But if you are putting off doing activities that you know
will bring you meaning and health, then that is a big deal.

• Visualize the kind of life you want—your dreams and desires—
then set goals, take action, and go for it! It is never too late.

• Life is short; eternity is not. It's time to celebrate getting older
while you learn to accentuate the positive. Savor every moment.
Celebrate the beauty, magic, and wonder of everyday life. Make
the most of this day, and the next, and the next.

CARPE DIEM:
Have you felt that sense of magic when everything aligns
just right in a day? What factors were present to make it
come together so well? Can you duplicate them today?

93.

ENJOY THE RIDE

"Enjoy life. There are no reruns."
— Shirl Lowery

• To decide how you want to live out your days, imagine the end. If you were in your last weeks of life, what would be important for you to do?

• There is a good chance that enjoying time with your loved ones is at the top of your list.

• Nothing brings home how precious life is more than the threat of death. A friend of ours was diagnosed with cancer, and for the first five days she didn't know whether she would live or die. A lot came to her during those days of unknowing. Two truths were instantly clear: The first was that she couldn't waste even one more minute on regret—she was precious and she needed to love and forgive herself for choices she made in the past. The second was to spend as much time as she could exchanging joy and love with her family and dearest friends. It struck her that joy—to feel it and to give it—is why we are here.

• Live these last years of your journey here on earth with the belief that every day is a gift. Fill it with the things that matter.

CARPE DIEM:
Today, call up someone who matters to you and plan a get-together.

94.

LIVE WITH PURPOSE

"Live your beliefs and you can turn the world around."
— Henry David Thoreau

- Living with purpose is choosing the direction of your life and heading in that direction. When you get sidetracked, as we all do, you refocus and set out again.

- Have you heard the recent term "intentional living"? It's a similar idea. Set your intentions for what you want, make the small choices each day that move you toward your intention, and you'll achieve it before you know it.

- What traits do you admire in people? Generosity? Warmth of spirit? Being real? Hold what it feels like to be this way, and move toward that feeling in your daily life.

- Happiness, health, and compassionate living: These are the things that most of us would like to experience in our twilight years. You can choose to strategically strive for these things. If you bounce through life without much thought, you may not achieve your hopes and dreams, and you will be left feeling restless and dissatisfied.

- Happiness is a choice, and being thankful for what you have in your life right now can allow you to be happy no matter what the circumstance, no matter what losses you have from aging. Set your intentions on happiness.

CARPE DIEM:
Set one intention right now and brainstorm
ways you can make it happen.

95.

INFUSE YOUR LIFE WITH MEANING

*"Nobody can go back and start a new beginning, but
anyone can start today and make a new ending."*
— Maria Robinson

- As we grow older, we often take inventory of our lives. What
  did we achieve? Who did we touch? What good did we do in the
  world? Was it all enough? If we are not careful, such an inventory
  can bring about self-judgment and shame.

- You only get one life to live. Take a deep breath and release any
  past pain, but hold on to past joys. Feel appreciation for them and
  bring them forward with you. It's time to travel light. Only pack
  the things you really care about—the ones that bring you meaning.

- Spend as little time possible fulfilling tasks and obligations and
  focus on what's important to you. Do those things as much as you
  can.

- Be daring—it is never too late! Maybe you always wanted to
  act in a play or help in a third-world country. If you still have
  the strength and stamina to do it, do it now! Don't hesitate. If
  your strength is low, modify your plan. For example, support a
  local theatre company by volunteering to take tickets or pass out
  programs.

- Infuse every day with meaning.

CARPE DIEM:
What brings you meaning? What would you still like to
explore? Make a list and put it on your refrigerator. Let it
be a reminder of how you want to spend your time.

96.

START A SPIRITUAL PRACTICE

*"We can never obtain peace in the outer world
until we make peace within ourselves."*
— Dalai Lama

• Many researchers find there is a strong connection between the mind, the spirit, and the body. As you age, tending to your spiritual needs will in turn benefit your mental and physical health as well.

• Starting a spiritual practice can be done at any age. Maybe you already attend worship services, are involved in a religious study group, read inspiring books, volunteer to help others, do yoga, or walk daily in nature. All these are spiritual practices. All invite your soul to come forward.

• Meditation, prayer, and religious ceremonies can calm and center you. They relieve stress and often set the world right.

• Prayer and meditation seem to be associated with improved immune system function and fewer episodes of chronic inflammation. People who identify themselves as religious and practice prayer and meditation have lower rates of depression.

• With the losses of aging, you can become imbalanced in mind, body, and spirit as you deal with the pain of your losses. You may have symptoms both physical and psychological, and you may even develop a sense of spiritual crisis. By attending to your spiritual needs on a regular basis you can work your way through this imbalance.

CARPE DIEM:
Which spiritual practice appeals to you? The intimacy
of prayer, meditation, or contemplation in nature? Or
does worshiping in a group lift you up? Decide on a
spiritual practice or two and add them to your life.

97.

PRAY

"If we could all hear one another's prayers, God might be relieved of some of His burdens."
— Ashleigh Brilliant

- Did you know that medical studies show that prayer can actually help people heal? Regular prayer can heal the mind, body, and soul.

- You don't have to adhere to any one faith or even consider yourself religious to pray. Think of prayer as a way to articulate your feelings, praise, thanks, and desires to your God, higher power, or the universe at large. Praying requires you to get in touch with your authentic self and form thoughts and words to express yourself. In this way, prayer heals and centers.

- If you are part of a place of worship and are going through a hard time, call and ask to be added to the community's prayer list. Feel this collective power.

- Every day, pray. Make it a habit. Consider it a daily release of your emotions and your soul. Pray for loved ones who have died. Pray for loved ones still alive. Pray for answers to your questions about life. Pray for direction. Let prayer help you set your intentions; forgive yourself and others; release any guilt, shame, or fear that you carry; and rejoice in your good luck and happiness.

CARPE DIEM:
Bow your head right now and say a silent prayer. If you are out of practice, don't worry. Let your thoughts flow naturally.

98.

HAVE FAITH

"Yes, you are as young as your faith, and as young as your hope, and as old as your despair."
— Douglas MacArthur

• Faith is such a powerful force in your life. You may have a strong religious faith that God will carry you through hard times and that someday you will be at God's side in heaven.

• Or maybe your faith is less defined by religion—maybe, over the years, you have adopted simple faiths, like, "Things often turns out well for me, as long as I face my fears and hardships head on." Or, "When I work hard, I can achieve what I set out to do" or even a faith that everything usually turns out fine. You may also have faith that people are inherently good. Most likely, you have faith in the love and relationships you experience with significant others

• Having faith in your spiritual beliefs, in the values that you hold dear, and in those you share life with is an important part of graceful aging.

• Without faith we accomplish little. We trust little. And we tend to accentuate the negative.

• Having faith in the order of the universe, yourself, and those around you creates peace in your soul.

CARPE DIEM:
What truisms or beliefs do you have faith in? Which people do you trust and respect? Make a list.

99.

CENTER YOURSELF

"If we live for tomorrow we will certainly be dead on arrival."
— Benjamin Sells

- Do you know what it feels like to be "centered"? The feeling of being centered is when everything lines up perfectly and you feel open, assured, blessed, and in touch with yourself and others.

- Centering yourself begins with a release of resistance. Your ego creates resistance. When you feel jealous, defensive, irritated, or negative, your ego has control. Being centered means releasing your ego and sitting in your soul and in your truth.

- When you are centered, things don't bother you. You have faith that everything is as it should be. You embrace all parts of yourself and see them as a perfect whole. You laugh at your foibles, and you feel your humanity.

- Breathing, praying, and taking breaks to be still can return you to center. If you feel the hassles of life—bills, aches and pains, loneliness—getting to you, stop and take a deep breath. Stand and stretch. Consciously release what's bothering you.

- Focus inward. When you are externally focused, little things bother you more than they should.

- Memorize what it feels like to be balanced. Let this be your goal, every day.

CARPE DIEM:

Which of your friends and family can you be your most authentic self with? Who lifts you up? Spend time with these people today.

100.

EMBRACE THE SEASONS OF LIFE

"Spring passes and one remembers one's innocence.
Summer passes and one remembers one's exuberance.
Autumn passes and one remembers one's reverence.
Winter passes and one remembers one's perseverance."

— Yoko Ono

• Like the passing of the seasons, life moves through various stages.
The spring of your youth passes into the summer of family life.
Family life passes into the autumn of midlife, and finally, you enter
the winter of older age.

• Remember, like the seasons of the year, each stage of life has its
own beauty. Each is magical in its own way.

• Relax into your winter. Equate perseverance with wisdom.
Life has taught you many valuable lessons, both practical and
spiritual. Now, more than ever, you are geared toward meaningful
experiences. You are settled in yourself and no longer question
who you are or what matters to you. If you can't do something,
or are not good at something else, so be it. You are who you are.
Relish in the beauty of this knowing. Sit with the stillness, like
fresh, fallen snow.

CARPE DIEM:

Relax into yourself. You have lived a full life thus far, and
there's more to come. Make it what you want it to be!

A FINAL WORD

Our Prayer For You

May the best book on how to age with grace and discernment be the life you write yourself. May you ask the questions and make the choices that help you befriend your unique journey with aging.

May you embrace what your life journey has been teaching you.

May the information and ideas shared in this book help you have meaning and purpose in the years yet to come.

May you come to understand that nothing is more fascinating than your own unique life story.

May the ideas outlined in these pages help program your head and your heart toward the best health and life balance possible.

As you grow older, may you be kind and gentle to yourself.

As you grow older, may you embrace both sorrow and joy.

As you grow older, may you be self-compassionate and allow your inner wisdom to touch the lives of those around you.

Blessings to you as you continue to explore your lessons learned, questions asked, and choices made.

Peace be with you!

FOR MORE INFORMATION

To receive a complete catalog of Dr. Alan Wolfelt's resources on healing in grief, please call (970) 226-6050. You can also order online at www. centerforloss.com. Click on Bookstore.

To learn more about Dr. Wolfelt's training seminars in Colorado or about bringing him to your community, please call (970) 226-6050 or visit www. centerforloss.com and click on "Attend a 4-Day Training in Colorado" or "Bring Dr. Wolfelt to Your Community."